The Spellmount Siegfried Line Series

Vol. 1 *West Wall: The Battle for Hitler's Siegfried Line* (available)
The story of Hitler's top secret line of fortifications which turned out to
be Germany's last line of defence in the final year of World War II

Vol. 2 *'44: In Combat from Normandy to the Ardennes* (available)
Eyewitness accounts of the attack from the beachhead to the Wall

Vol. 3 *Bloody Aachen* (available)
The first major battle for the most impregnable part of the West Wall

Vol. 4 *The Battle of Hurtgen Forest* (available)
The officially covered-up defeat of 12 US Divisions;
the lead up to the Battle of the Bulge

Vol. 5 *Ardennes: The Secret War* (available)
The secret preparations for the 'surprise attack' in the Ardennes –
the US's 'Gettysburg of the 20th century'

Vol. 6 *Decision at St Vith* (available)
The decisive battle for the West Wall frontier town that broke
the back of the German assault

Vol. 7 *The Other Battle of the Bulge: Operation* Northwind (available)
The unknown battle fought by the US 7th Army –
the 'Forgotten Army' – in Alsace

Vol. 8 *Patton's Last Battle* (available)
Patton's major breakthrough in the West Wall,
before his fall from grace and his accidental death

Vol. 9 *Bounce the Rhine*
The British role in breaching the West Wall,
and the triumphant crossing of the Rhine

BOUNCE
THE RHINE

by

Charles Whiting

SPELLMOUNT
Staplehurst

British Library Cataloguing in Publication Data:
A catalogue record for this book is available
from the British Library

Copyright © Charles Whiting 1985, 2002

ISBN 1-86227-151-8

First published in 1985 by
Leo Cooper in association with Secker & Warburg Ltd

This edition first published in the UK in 2002 by
Spellmount Limited
The Old Rectory
Staplehurst
Kent TN12 0AZ

Tel: 01580 893730
Fax: 01580 893731
E-mail: enquiries@spellmount.com
Website: www.spellmount.com

1 3 5 7 9 8 6 4 2

The right of Charles Whiting to be identified
as the author of this work has been asserted by him
in accordance with the Copyright, Designs
and Patents Act 1988

Printed and bound in Great Britain by
TJ International Ltd, Padstow, Cornwall

CONTENTS

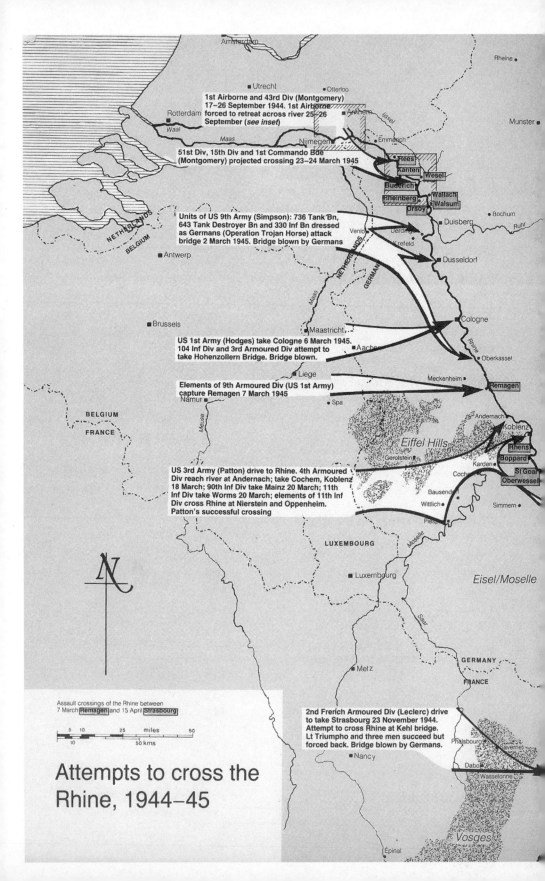

1st Airborne and 43rd Div (Montgomery) 17–26 September 1944. 1st Airborne forced to retreat across river 25–26 September (see inset)

51st Div, 15th Div and 1st Commando Bde (Montgomery) projected crossing 23–24 March 1945

Units of US 9th Army (Simpson): 736 Tank Bn, 643 Tank Destroyer Bn and 330 Inf Bn dressed as Germans (Operation Trojan Horse) attack bridge 2 March 1945. Bridge blown by Germans

US 1st Army (Hodges) take Cologne 6 March 1945. 104 Inf Div and 3rd Armoured Div attempt to take Hohenzollern Bridge. Bridge blown.

Elements of 9th Armoured Div (US 1st Army) capture Remagen 7 March 1945

US 3rd Army (Patton) drive to Rhine. 4th Armoured Div reach river at Andernach; take Cochem, Koblenz 18 March; 90th Inf Div take Mainz 20 March; 11th Inf Div take Worms 20 March; elements of 11th Inf Div cross Rhine at Nierstein and Oppenheim. Patton's successful crossing

2nd French Armoured Div (Leclerc) drive to take Strasbourg 23 November 1944. Attempt to cross Rhine at Kehl bridge. Lt Triumpho and three men succeed but forced back. Bridge blown by Germans.

Assault crossings of the Rhine between 7 March Remagen and 15 April Strasbourg

5 10   25   miles   50
10   50 kms

Attempts to cross the Rhine, 1944–45

NETHERLANDS

BELGIUM

GERMANY

BELGIUM
FRANCE

LUXEMBOURG

Eisel/Moselle

GERMANY
FRANCE

Vosges

Amsterdam
Rhine
Utrecht
Otterloo
Rotterdam
Arnhem
Munster
Waal
Maas
Nijmegen
Emmerich
Iissel
Rees
Xanten
Wesel
Buderich
Wallach
Rheinberg
Walsum
Orsoy
Bochum
Duisberg
Ruhr
Venlo
Uerding
Krefeld
Antwerp
Dusseldorf
Brussels
Maastricht
Aachen
Cologne
Oberkassel
Liege
Meckenheim
Namur
Remagen
Spa
Andernach
Koblenz
Eiffel Hills
Rhens
Gerolstein
Boppard
Karden
St Goar
Cochem
Oberwessel
Bausenden
Wittlich
Simmern
Piesport
Luxembourg
Metz
Moselle
Saar
Nancy
Phalsbourg
Saverne
Dabo
Wasselonne
Épinal

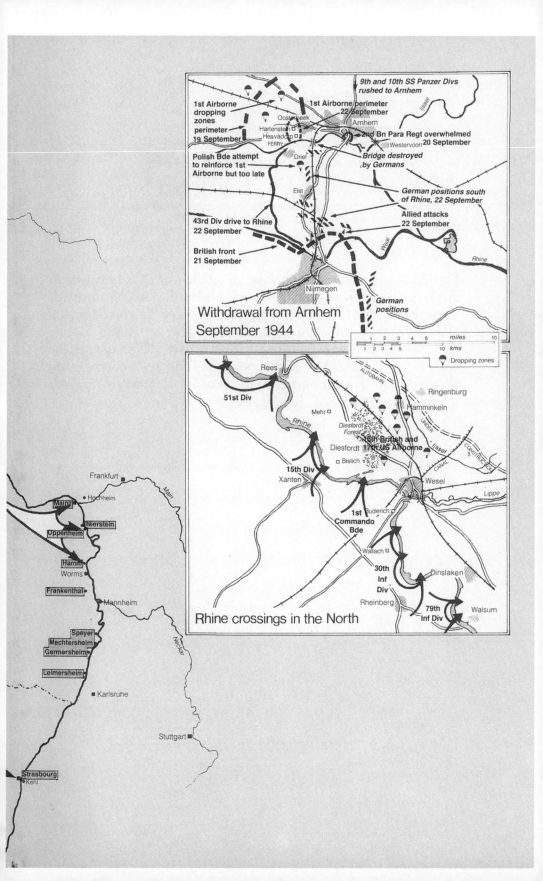

Withdrawal from Arnhem September 1944

9th and 10th SS Panzer Divs rushed to Arnhem

1st Airborne dropping zones perimeter 19 September

1st Airborne perimeter 22 September

2nd Bn Para Regt overwhelmed 20 September

Oosterbeek

Arnhem

Hartenstein

Heavadorp

FERRY

Westervoort

Driel

Bridge destroyed by Germans

Polish Bde attempt to reinforce 1st Airborne but too late

Elst

German positions south of Rhine, 22 September

Allied attacks 22 September

43rd Div drive to Rhine 22 September

British front 21 September

Waal

Rhine

Nijmegen

German positions

Ijssel

miles 1 2 3 4 5 10
kms 1 2 3 4 5 10

Dropping zones

Rhine crossings in the North

Rees

51st Div

AUTOBAHN

Ringenburg

Hamminkeln

Rhine

Mehr

Diesfordt Forest

UNDER

18th British and 17th US Airborne

Diesfordt

Ijssel

CONSTRUCTION

15th Div

Bislich

Wesel

Xanten

CANAL

1st Commando Bde

Buderich

Lippe

Wallach

30th Inf Div

Dinslaken

79th Inf Div

Rheinberg

Walsum

Frankfurt

Hochheim

Main

Mainz

Nierstein

Oppenheim

Hamm

Worms

Frankenthal

Mannheim

Neckar

Speyer

Mechtersheim

Germersheim

Leimersheim

Karlsruhe

Stuttgart

Strasbourg

Kehl

ACKNOWLEDGEMENTS

I would like to thank the following for all their invaluable assistance in the preparation of this book: the Stadtarchiv of the towns of Oppenheim, Rees, Wesel and Speyer; Messers Thixton, Bridges, Duke, Pennock and Burrows of the paras; ex-Royal Marine Commando Mr Cosgrave; former members of the "Nijmegen Home Guard", in particular Mr Jack Frame; Group Captain Winterbotham; Charles Bedford and his mates of the 53rd Division; Major Gill; Mr Tom Stubbs of the USAF, Bitburg, Germany.

INTRODUCTION

Sometimes the thick pillars of smoke and flame were the funeral pyres of brave men and we who report this war have a duty to the dead equally with the living to tell things as they are, stripped at times of the glamour and the glory.
R. W. Thompson (describing the airborne landing on the Rhine, March 24th, 1945)

Once, in a moment of self-mockery, he had called himself "a broken-down ex-cavalryman". Six months later, in February 1945, he was exactly that. His guts were wrapped in a mass of grubby bandages; he had been wounded in the thigh and under the eye; and for nearly half a year he had been on the run from the Germans, living on a semi-starvation diet, a mere six hundred calories a day.

But now he was coming home, the last of them to escape. Members of the Dutch Resistance had rowed him across the river last night – the same river over which they had so confidently flown the previous September. On the Allied side he had been welcomed with mugs of "sarnt-major's char" and whisky by his friends of the 11th Hussars, the 'Cherrypickers', in the comfortable jumble of the British Army in the field, before falling into an exhausted sleep in their CO's bed.

Next morning he was on the road heading south to the airfield where the Field-Marshal's C-47 would be waiting for him. Everywhere he looked there were British Army convoys moving up to the new front in Germany. Once again they were going to attempt what he and all those thousands – long dead, or vanished into the prison cage – had failed to do.

But this time, as the last survivor relaxed in the back of the big

Humber staff car, he could almost feel victory in the air. "From the apparently endless quantities of new equipment, the well-fed faces of the troops in their new-looking uniforms, and the bounding air of confidence over everyone and everything, it was easy to see where final victory would be."[1]

His old chief received him at his Headquarters with a warm welcome and a splendid dinner: oysters, wine and "other marvellous things to eat". For the first time in months the escaper ate a meal that was definitely well over six hundred calories.

Afterwards his ascetic former chief, with his sharp beaky face and piercing blue eyes, indicated the decanter on the table in front of them. "Come along," he barked in that familiar high-pitched voice of his. "Have some of this cold tea stuff. Some of you chaps seem to like it."

The escaper's mouth nearly dropped open in surprise. Here was the notorious, teetotal, non-smoking Field-Marshal Montgomery actually pressing him to have a glass of sherry!

Thus refreshed and relaxed, the escaper and Montgomery began to talk. They talked about Montgomery's plans and preparations for the great operations in Germany to come. They also talked a little about what had happened that September, but not much. What could a "broken-down ex-cavalryman" say that would make sense of it all? He had gone in with a strength of about 1,000 parachute infantry; fewer than 100 had come out – and he had not been one of them. Besides, Montgomery was not interested in past defeats. "The Master", as his adoring young staff called him behind his back, had his eyes firmly on the future – and victory.

Next day the escaper was flown back to England in the Army Commander's own aeroplane. That same night the BBC broadcast a cryptic coded message to the Dutch Underground in Occupied Holland: "*The Grey Goose has gone.*"

It had indeed. Brigadier John Hackett, that "broken-down ex-cavalryman", the last commander of the decimated British 4th Parachute Brigade, was home from Arnhem at last. Montgomery had drawn a line under his first defeat on the Rhine. Now, six months later, he was aiming for victory on the same great river that had thwarted him so bloodily at Arnhem ...

Not far from Switzerland's border with Italy, two glacier-fed mountain streams rush eastwards for a few miles before they meet to form the River Rhine. Still little more than a mountain torrent, it flows north along the Austrian border until it reaches Lake Constance. At the western side of the lake it falls seventy feet over the celebrated Schaffenhausen Falls and winds between Switzerland and Germany to the frontier town of Basle. Here it turns sharply north and starts to grow in width until it becomes half a mile across, the natural boundary that separates France from Germany.

On and on it winds, past the fortress cities created by the Romans when this was the furthermost border of their great empire against the Barbarians, receiving the tributory waters of the Neckar, the Main, the Moselle. Then suddenly it swings generally north once more and enters the great gorge that constricts its passage. On and on for 850 miles, until finally it flows into Holland to be lost in a delta, one channel wending past Arnhem to Rotterdam and from thence to the sea.

In Roman times the river formed a barrier against those strange wild peoples of the east, the *Limes*, until the massive Germanic migration known as *die Voelkerwanderung* finally swept it away and the Barbarians swamped the whole of Europe, conquering even mighty Rome itself.

In the Middle Ages the Rhine flowed through the "Priests' Lane", the richest part of Europe, dominated by powerful German bishops whose wealth was founded on profits and gifts from those who controlled the commerce on Western Europe's most important trade route. As the centuries passed, however, the Rhine ceased to be a fief of the Church. Instead it became the prime bone of contention between French imperialists and German nationalists. From the late seventeenth century until the twentieth century, battles raged up and down it for its possession. "The Rhine is our river and *not* our frontier!" bellowed those early scarfaced students, thumping out the tune of that bombastic "*Die Wacht am Rhein*" with their beer-mugs on the scrubbed wooden tables.

It was in this period that Baedeker discovered the Rhine as an early tourist attraction – the "romantic Rhine" of the guidebooks. It became the kindly old "Father Rhine" of the newly revived *Karnivalgesellschaften*, the pre-Lenten festival marked with parades and revelry – and plenty of beer and wine. The old legends were rediscovered, those Germanic sagas from the dawn of recorded history: Siegfried and the Ring of the Nibelungen; Attila the Hun and Kriemhild; the Lorelei; and all the rest of those fabled figures, half-based on fact.

In the end, the Western Allies put a stop to the continual squab-
bling between France and Germany for possession of the Rhine by
occupying the west bank of the river in 1918. Or so they thought. But
once again, in the years that followed the *Versaillesdiktat*, the Rhine
became a vital symbol for the Germans: a symbol of unity and
national awakening under the new leader – Adolf Hitler.

In 1930 the last of three Western Allies withdrew its troops from
the Occupied Rhineland. Six years later the soldiers of the newly
recreated Wehrmacht goose-stepped through cheering delirious
throngs of citizens in Mainz, Cologne, Koblenz and half a dozen other
Rhenish cities on the West Bank. Once again the Rhine was no longer
Germany's border but her river.

Almost immediately a security curtain descended upon the Rhine
area, virtually as impenetrable as that fabled fog with which the
warriors of the Nibelungen could surround themselves once they had
placed the *Tarnkappe* on their blond heads.

Germany's border with France, Luxembourg and Belgium became
the "red zone" for strangers; it was turned into a *Sperrgebiet*, a restric-
ted area. In the newly regained territory west of the Rhine, training
camps or *Adolf Hitler Kasernen* (they were invariably named after the
Führer) were springing up everywhere. Conscripts came flooding in to
swell the 100,000-man army of the old *Versaillesdiktat* – from
500,000, to a million. *But to do what?*

Both French and British were in the dark. By 1938 they had hardly a
single agent still operating in the Rhineland. Commandant Georges
Ronin of the French Deuxième Bureau tried to find out from the air.
He bribed Air France flying over the Rhine to take hasty snapshots as
they crossed it. But when the German authorities ordered that all
foreign planes had to fly at over 8,000 feet this source dried up;
cameras could not operate effectively at such altitudes.

Ronin tried another approach. Flying along the French side of the
Rhine, his cameraman – an ancient, bearded and very frightened
Parisian portrait photographer, operating an old-fashioned wooden
camera – took pictures of the opposite side. But the results were poor,
and in the end Ronin passed the buck to his British opposite number,
Fred Winterbotham of MI6.

The tall blond Englishman succeeded where the Frenchman had
failed. In effect Winterbotham created the first U-2 spy-plane in the
shape of a Lockheed 12-A, piloted by Australian adventurer Sidney

Cotton.[2] Together the two of them discovered that if the heat from the cabin was led to the plane's three cameras, it would prevent the lenses from fogging up. As a result the Lockheed could fly at the height ordered by the Germans: a height from which they thought it was impossible to take photographs.

In July 1939, on one of his last flights, Cotton even succeeded in getting two unsuspecting senior Luftwaffe commanders to take photographs of top-secret German installations on the Rhine for him. During the course of the Frankfurt Air Show, while Cotton was demonstrating the plane to the two Germans, General Kesselring and General Milch, Kesselring asked to fly the plane himself. Cotton graciously agreed and suggested casually that they should fly towards Mannheim on the Rhine, Mannheim being an area that Winterbotham particularly wanted to know about as there were some Luftwaffe bases there.

While Kesselring focused his attention on the controls, Cotton seized his opportunity. He turned on the cameras.

After some time Kesselring noticed a green light on the control panel flashing on and off. "What is that light for?" he asked.

"It is a special device, *Herr General*", Cotton lied glibly, "to show the petrol flow to the engine."

In fact, the green light indicated that the cameras were functioning correctly – but Kesselring accepted Cotton's explanation and flew on, photographing the first hard evidence of what the Germans were doing along the mysterious Rhine in the last summer of peace.

Five years later, as the last commander-in-chief of the Wehrmacht in the West, it was the same General Kesselring who would be given the task of leading the third Reich's last-ditch stand on that same river!

Nearly half a decade would elapse before the Western Allies could make use of Cotton's information and all the rest of the intelligence they had collected in the intervening period about the Rhine and its defences. Twice in 1944 attempts were made to cross "Father Rhine" by force: the first was made by Montgomery's Britons; the second was by Frenchmen under the command of a maverick general who wanted nothing to do with his own French Army. Both failed.

By the early spring of 1945 the British and the Canadians – and the French too – were preparing to have another go. But by this time there were other contenders for the glory and honour of successfully crossing Western Europe's greatest river – the Americans.

PART I

Defeat on the Rhine

Casualties have been grievous but for those who mourn there is the consolation that the sacrifice was not needlessly demanded ... Now I shall not hazard a guess as to when the end [of the war] will come.

Winston Churchill, September 28th, 1944

ONE

Dawn came reluctantly that Monday morning, as if Nature herself was hesitating to throw light on the war-torn world below. But by now the big General had made his decision. Already the German guns had commenced thundering once more and shells were dropping all around the battered hotel that had been his HQ for the last terrible week. Here and there one of his mortars on the perimeter took up the challenge, answering with a thick, throaty crump. But the General knew it was hopeless. He was completely outgunned and his once proud division had been reduced from over 10,000 men to a mere 2,500, many of them wounded. If he were to save the survivors they would have to withdraw this day.

At ten o'clock he assembled what was left of his staff. "Gentlemen," he told them without any attempt at drama or pathos, "we are to clear out tonight."

The weary staff officers had been expecting the announcement for over twenty-four hours. Yet their faces were bitter at the thought of all the good men, each one a volunteer, who had died for nothing.

The General, who had once studied the classic withdrawal from Gallipoli in World War One for a promotion exam, explained that he would use that as the model for his own withdrawal. He envisaged a slow retreat, under cover of darkness, from the northern sector of his hard-pressed perimeter, moving down each flank and systematically pulling the defenders out until it came to the turn of the men dug in closest to the river. "In effect," he wrote later after it was all over, "I planned the withdrawal like the collapse of a paper bag. I wanted small parties stationed at strategic places to give the impression we were still there, all the while pulling downward and along each flank."

In front of them, now that the great decision had been made, there were nine long hours till darkness. Even now the snap-and-crackle of small arms fire from outside the Dutch hotel indicated that the SS infantry were attacking his perimeter yet once again. During this period, the General told his officers, they would have to carry out their duties as normally as they could. Radio traffic would be maintained. Prisoners would be guarded as strictly as ever by the MPs. The men in the line would keep up their defensive fire. And above all, he emphasized, the strictest security would have to be ensured. He did not want any para taken prisoner by the Germans this day to babble to the Boche. Besides, once the tired, hungry paras manning the line knew they were going out, they would commence "to look over their shoulder", as he put it, thus reducing their effectiveness. And, he snapped, he wanted no more of those unreasoning panics they had all witnessed over the last few days when men had thrown away their weapons and simply fled to the rear. The 1st British Airborne Division was going to leave Arnhem as proudly as it had arrived ...

The news began to filter down from the staff to the soldiers, as the big General's few remaining guns beat off yet another determined attack by SS panzer-grenadiers and tanks. Some were shocked by the decision to withdraw. Major George Powell, fighting on the top of the perimeter, thought it was "an appalling blow. I thought of all the men who had died and then I thought the whole effort had been a waste."[1]

Private Dukes, dug in at the shattered Oosterbeek Church, took it stoically. As the men around him tossed coins to decide who would stay behind and cover their retreat, with the *winner* of the toss being the loser, he reflected that he'd been through it all before at Dunkirk. To him it seemed that this would be "no worse, but no better" than that terrible evacuation of four years before.[2]

Glider pilot Louis Hagen's CO "fairly radiated optimism" as he told his sergeants that they were pulling out. It would be an orderly operation, he said; all sections would leave their posts on the perimeter at a specified time with all their arms and ammunition. Thus encouraged, the NCOs – who were going to act as guides for the rest of the division – wolfed down all their remaining rations; they'd need the energy for the long hazardous night that lay ahead.

And, even in defeat, bull reigned supreme. Private Harding's sergeant ordered him to go over to the hotel HQ. Here another sergeant met him and snapped: "There's an old plastic razor over there."

Harding stared at the brown plastic issue razor in weary bewilderment. "You get yourself a dry shave," the NCO barked. "Hurry up! We're crossing the river – and by God, we're going back looking like British soldiers!"[3]

The same sentiment was shared by Colonel Ian Murray, who commanded the Glider Pilot Regiment. Handing his razor to Major Toler of the same regiment, he said, "We're getting out. We don't want the army to think we're a bunch of tramps."[4]

Dutifully the Major started to shave, as the German guns thundered and the torrential rain lashed the shell-pocked walls of the hotel. They were going out, washed and shaved, in the best traditions of the British Army.

As the heavy guns of the British XXX Corps crashed into action on the other side of the great river, the big General, his face blackened like all the rest and his boots muffled with rags, visited the wounded in the hotel cellar. Despite the recent truce which had allowed them to evacuate most of the original wounded, it was crowded again with fresh casualties, packed together on the straw, the blood staining through their makeshift bandages, their shattered limbs held by crude splints fashioned from bayonets, chair legs, anything that would do the job.

Sadly the General passed through their ranks, saying goodbye to those still conscious, nodding to those snoring heavily with the morphia that had been pumped into them to still the pain. Not one of them was over the age of twenty-five. Now these bold young men, who had so valiantly served him and the man who had sent him on this impossible adventure, Field-Marshal Montgomery, were to be left behind to an uncertain fate. How the SS would treat them was anybody's guess.

He turned to go, eyes still full of their pain-racked faces in the flickering yellow light of the candles. Just then a soldier struggled to prop himself up against the dirty white wall of the cellar. "I hope you make it, sir," he said. The big General could have cried.

Long columns of defeated survivors started to trudge through the pouring rain towards the river, where they were to be taken out in boats. Some were too exhausted to care very much any more; they simply plodded blindly forward in the inky darkness – right into the hands of the startled Germans who surrounded them. Others were still full of spirit and fight.

Sergeant Hagen's CO was absolutely confident that he knew the route, as his men trudged through the night, although Hagen could see that the path was becoming increasingly difficult to follow through the dense Dutch wood. "We'll make it," he kept whispering to Hagen. "Don't worry. Stick to me."

Miraculously they found their first landmark: a shattered farm-house. Here, Hagen knew, they would have to branch left down a lane. Suddenly a German machine gun cracked into action to their immediate front. The glider pilots halted, crouched in the pelting rain … But the Germans weren't firing at them. They pushed on, only to find their path blocked by a fence.

Abruptly a bareheaded officer, who had been wounded, loomed up out of the rain-swept darkness. "*Germans!*" he panted. "Ambushed my men!"

But the captain in charge of the glider pilots didn't lose his head. He ordered his men to turn about to find another escape route. "The men were remarkably silent and there was no shuffling or pushing," Hagen remembered afterwards.[6] Weary but uncomplaining, those hundreds of young men simply turned in their path and found another way through to the river, heads bowed against the constant rain.

Eventually the first of them had reached the muddy bank. Above their heads, a tremendous barrage put up by the XXX Corps' massed guns plastered the German positions and deadened any noise the escapers made. But already the SS had grown suspicious. They were pushing in patrols on all sides. Their mortars – the dreaded "moaning minnies" – were also cracking into action, screaming through the darkness with that blood-curdling, baleful howl. The escapers started to take casualties.

Hagen's glider pilot party was now crossing an open meadow, lit by the fitful pink light of gunfire. The ground was littered with dead bodies, sprawled out in the extravagant attitudes of those who have met a violent death. Hagen came across a wounded para begging piteously not to be left behind. Hagen and a comrade tried to lift the man, but he screamed in pain. Alarmed and worried that his screams would attract German fire, they lowered him hurriedly.

Hagen stumbled on towards the river, almost tripping over the fallen bodies. Some of the wounded men were trying to drag themselves the last few yards across the meadow to the river bank, sobbing aloud with the effort and the pain. "Feverish pleading eyes looked up towards me," Hagen recalled later, "arms clutched around my legs. It seemed that all the wounded were frenzied by the fear of being left behind."[7]

Hagen shared that fear – especially as he was a German-born Jew, who had already spent some time in a concentration camp back in the thirties. Now, for the first time since he'd landed at Arnhem, he panicked. "I dragged limp bodies along towards the beach – I ran round in circles searching for someone in command and pleaded with uninjured men to give me a hand – I vomited and fainted."[8]

Suddenly an authoritative voice ordered him to stop his antics. He was to continue with the rest to the river. The wounded would be left behind where they lay. A doctor would stay with them. That firm steady voice brought him back to his senses. "Exhausted and dazed by my impotence and the ghastliness of the scene," as he recorded later, Hagen staggered forwards to the river.[9]

Stanley Maxted, the gravel-voiced Canadian correspondent of the BBC, emerged from the woods onto the river bank and "felt as naked as if I were in Piccadilly Circus in my pyjamas because of the glow of the fires across the river. The machine-gun and general bombardment had never let up. We lay down flat in the mud and rain and stayed that way for two hours till the sentry beyond the hedge on the bank told us to move up over the dyke and be taken across. Mortaring started now and I was fearful for those who were already over on the bank. I guessed it was pretty bad for them. After what seemed a nightmare of an age, we got our turn.'[10]

Maxted slithered down the muddy bank into the icy water with the rest, while the night sky was torn to shreds by tracer fire, ripping over their heads. A dark shadow of a boat nosed its way out of the fog of war and Maxted suddenly heard a voice that was "sheer music" to his ears: "Ye'll have to step lively, boys, it ain't healthy here!"

Some of the men began to panic. Glider pilot Wade arrived at the river, having lost many a comrade during the nightmarish trip, to find a chaotic scene of tension and fear. As he recalled after the war, "Wounded were being helped to the front. Others felt they'd never make it. A boat would leave, dissolve in the murk and might not return. Understandably, those left were an edgy bunch."[11]

Indeed, many of them were so edgy that they refused to wait for room in a boat. They simply plunged into the water, not realizing that it had a current of up to eight knots. They were drowned by the score.

By now the beachhead was under direct machine-gun fire. The men surged forward to the boats crewed by Canadian engineers. Officers and NCOs tried to hold them back. In vain Corporal Harris of the 1st

Parachute Battalion later recalled "hundreds and hundreds waiting to get across. Boats were swamped by the weight of the numbers of men trying to board."[12]

Others preserved their traditional good humour. Glider Pilot Cardy remembers someone shouting, "Seats at one and sixpence! Ninepence standing!"[13] It was a corny old joke, familiar from the long wartime cinema queues, but it helped to relieve the strain for a moment, allowing the men to get a hold of themselves, even though the Germans were thrusting ever closer now.

But as the Germans pressed home their attack, fewer and fewer boats were returning from the far bank to pick up the survivors still waiting to be rescued. Panic set in. "It was impossible to regulate the number of passengers carried by the boats at a time," Canadian engineer Major Tucker reported later. "Men panicked and stormed onto the boats, in some cases capsizing them. In many cases they had to be beaten off or threatened with shooting to avoid having the boats swamped. With the approach of dawn this condition became worse. They were so afraid that daylight would force us to cease our ferrying before they could be rescued."

In a break between mortar barrages, Hagen and his comrades had joined the long line of men waiting in the soaking darkness for the last of the boats. All around them lay the dead and wounded, abandoned there in the mud like sodden, broken dolls.

A boat appeared out of the rain. It took a mere ten men out of the hundred standing in line in front of the sergeant. He crouched with the rest in the squelching mud, frozen and miserable. The "moaning minnies" started to howl again. Suddenly he made his decision. He was no longer prepared to be "heroic, playing at Dunkirk". He turned to his CO and announced that he was going to try to swim across.

Above the malevolent howl of the multiple mortars the CO shouted back that he was going to do the same – and by the time Hagen, a good swimmer, had slung his boots around his neck, the CO was already in the river and swimming strongly for the opposite bank, clearly visible in the lurid, unnatural light.

Hagen plunged into the water. To his horror he found he couldn't catch up. The current was sweeping his CO rapidly downstream. But he had no time to worry about the CO. Suddenly he found he wasn't making proper strokes. He was gasping and choking for breath.

"Like a flash it came to me that this was the one fatal thing to do and the best possible way to drown."

By an effort of sheer willpower, he forced himself to turn on his back and float while he recovered his breath; then systematically he began to divest himself of his Sten gun, smock, personal gear, even his Army paybook. Now finally he was ready to swim. "The difference was marvellous. I felt like I had when I'd been bathing a fortnight ago in the Thames ... I looked around for Captain Z [his CO] but there was no sign of him at all ..."[14]

"Right – this party!" the subdued Canadian voice hissed. Wearily the big General rose from the mud. One by one the HQ party squeezed aboard the assault boat. It set off immediately. Corporal Hancock, the General's batman, who had been with him right through the fighting in the Desert, tried to get aboard. "Let go!" someone yelled at him. The undersized batman ignored the order; he scrambled into the boat. Tracer was zig-zagging across the river like flights of angry red hornets. Skilfully the Canadian at the tiller dodged the bullets. Suddenly the engine spluttered. The exhausted HQ party stared at each other in horror. Slowly the craft came to a stop in mid-river, drifting with the current, while all around them the slugs cut the air.

Frantic with desperation the Canadian crew struggled to restart the motor. Finally, after what seemed to the tense General "an absolute age", they succeeded. With a great roar, the engine burst into noisy life. Minutes later the prow of the little craft bumped into a wooden barrier. "All right, let's be having you!" a tough voice commanded. Hastily the HQ party dropped over the side and began to labour up a steep bank towards the dark shapes waiting for them in the pouring rain above. The General took a grip on the slippery concreted bank and with a grunt attempted to heave up his fourteen stone bulk. There was an ominous snap. "*Blast!*" he cursed.

"What is it, sir?" his ADC enquired anxiously.

"It's all right," the General replied testily. "It's only my braces."

Unshaven, his battledress torn and soaked, holding up his trousers with irritated dignity, the General had at last reached safety. He was not, as he later recorded bitterly, received "with any warmth".

It was, in fact, some time later before the General met his Corps Commander. The General had been offered clean dry clothing, but he had refused; he wanted his Corps Commander to see him as he was, soaked, worn and "stinking to high heaven".

The Corps Commander, General "Boy" Browning, an ex-Guards officer, appeared as if "he had just come off parade rather than from his bed in the middle of a battle".

The General told him simply: "I'm sorry – things did not turn out as well as I had hoped."

"You did all you could," Browning assured him. Then he sent the General off to bed. But sleep was impossible. "There were too many things," he remembered later, "on my mind and my conscience."

There were indeed. His division had been decimated. After nine days of sacrifice, he had lost 1,200 men dead and 6,642 missing, wounded or captured. Of the three brigadiers in the division, only one had returned. Three battalion commanders were dead; four were wounded and prisoners-of-war; one was wounded and on the run behind German lines at the other side of the river. Twenty-five medical officers had remained behind with the wounded. Only two of the division's fifteen padres had returned. Four battalions of airborne infantry ceased to exist . . . Thus the litany of defeat went on.

Sergeant Hagen was one of the lucky ones. Safely across the river he now found himself in a long queue of wet, shivering paras filing past tables at which sat doctors, who prescribed drugs or treatment for most of the escapees. Hagen came level and an orderly painted a figure on his forehead and prepared to give him a morphia injection.

Hagen protested that he hadn't been wounded.

Curtly the orderly answered, "I'm treating for shock here. You'll feel fine in a minute." He continued with his preparations.

But Hagen had had enough. He pushed the medic out of the way. A struggle ensued. A doctor rushed up and Hagen told him he wasn't shocked, only cold and wet. Another orderly was brought up. Together they removed Hagen's soaked, bloody uniform and slung it on a pile of wet, blood-stained garments in the middle of the room, then wrapped him in blankets and sat him in front of a flickering oil stove. A cup of very sweet tea was thrust into his frozen hands and someone shoved a lighted cigarette between his lips. Hagen felt he was "in paradise".

Not all the "blood-bathed heroes", as the Press back home was already calling them, were welcomed back so warmly. After seeing the General, Browning jumped into his jeep and drove to the river himself. There he made a speech, congratulating some of the survivors on "the show they had put up". But on his way back to Corps HQ, followed by an escort of five paras armed with tommy guns, he passed a dazed survivor who failed to salute. Browning's jeep squealed to a stop and an aide was sent running to the soldier. Why had the para failed to salute the commanding general, demanded the aide.

"But I haven't seen a general for a long time, sir," the soldier protested. "And besides, I wasn't looking."

The aide didn't like the soldier's answer. He doubled back to his immaculate Corps Commander sitting in the jeep. They conferred for a few seconds, then the aide returned to where the para waited, standing rigidly to attention in dumb apprehension.

"General Browning says," the aide snapped, "that you are not to be allowed to wear your red beret for the next fourteen days!"[15]

It was almost over. All night long, Warrant Officer John Sharp of the 2nd Parachute Battalion had stood in the rain asking the soaked survivors, "Has anyone seen the 2nd Battalion? ... Has anyone seen the 2nd Battalion?" And always the answer was "no", for very few men had escaped from those gallant six hundred men who had defended the vital bridge across the river.

At dawn the first man stumbled in. All morning Sharp waited and waited till in the end the river was empty. No one else was coming. Now he could make his final count. A total of seventeen men had escaped from the slaughter of the 2nd Battalion. As the hard-boiled NCO remembered long afterwards, "I don't think I was the only one with tears in my eyes ..."[16]

All was silent. Cora Balthussen who had been wounded in the battle could see the smoke rising from the ruins of Arnhem on the other side of the river. But that was all. The noise of battle had ceased. Curious, she decided the cycle into Driel to find out what was going on.

The little town was almost deserted. Only a few Polish and British paras hung around smoking next to their jeeps. Obviously the Allies were pulling out. Soon the Germans would be coming back.

As the Dutch woman approached a small group of soldiers to ask them what was happening, the bell in Driel's shell-damaged church steeple started to toll. She looked up, startled. Up in the belfry there was a British para, his head bound with a bandage.

"What happened?" she called out.

"It's all over," he answered. "All over. We pulled out. We're the last lot."

"Why are you ringing the bell?" she asked as the soldier kicked it once more.

As the echo of the tolling bell died away, the para looked down at her and answered simply, "It seemed like the right thing to do . . ."[17]

2

The defeated commander had one more meeting to undertake on the Continent before he would be allowed to return home and decent obscurity. He was ordered to meet the man who had engineered the bold operation that had ended so disastrously, the newly created Field-Marshal Bernard Law Montgomery.

At teatime on that Thursday, two days after he had been rescued, he reported at Montgomery's HQ, just outside the Dutch town of Eindhoven. There he was met by one of Montgomery's aides, a worried man, who told the General that two of the Field-Marshal's pet rabbits had escaped from their cage. The General did not respond; he thought it wiser to keep his opinions on the rabbits to himself.

Montgomery greeted the General in his usual crisp, businesslike manner. If the Field-Marshal felt any disappointment at the failure of his bold plan to cross the great river that separated him from the "guts" and the "heart" of the Third Reich (respectively, the Ruhr and Berlin), he did not show it. Thrusting out his skinny hand, he snapped, "Good to see you got back all right. Come and sit down and let's talk it over."[18]

Thus the two generals who had been responsible for more British casualties than on D-Day itself, sat down in the warm spring sunshine in front of the Field-Marshal's celebrated caravan, which had accompanied him all the way through Africa, Sicily, Italy, France, Belgium and now Holland, and discussed what had happened at Montgomery's first disastrous attempt to do what he had confidently proclaimed he would do only three weeks before: to "bounce the Rhine".

Drinking weak tea and enjoying the pleasant autumn sunshine, the General got it off his broad chest, explaining what had gone wrong in those nine terrible days of Arnhem, prompted by curt questions from the Field-Marshal. That evening the two men had dinner together in the mess tent, with Montgomery retiring after his glass of warm milk at his usual early hour. Next morning the General was taking a breath of air before leaving to fly back home when Montgomery came out of his caravan flourishing a piece of paper. "This I would like to give you," he declared briskly. "I shall issue a copy to my public relations officer as well."

The General saw that the paper was typed, but Montgomery assured him he had written it first in his own hand that very morning. Seated in the plane later, the General read the Field-Marshal's statement, which was written in the form of a personal letter to him. In part it read:

"I also want to express to you my own admiration and the admiration of us all in 21st Army Group for the magnificent fighting spirit that your Division displayed in battle against great odds ... There is no shadow of a doubt that, had you failed, operations elsewhere would have been gravely compromised. You did not fail and all is well elsewhere.

"In the annals of the British Army there are many glorious deeds. In our Army we have always drawn great strength and inspiration from past traditions and endeavoured to live up to the high standard of those who have gone before. But there can be few episodes more glorious than the epic of Arnhem ...

"So long as we have in armies of the British Empire officers and men who will do as you have done, then we can indeed look forward with complete confidence to the future. In years to come it will be a great thing for a man to be able to say: *I fought at Arnhem!*"[19]

The General's reaction is not recorded. But he went home "a hero" and "was personally decorated by the King",[20] noted General Gavin bitterly – for Gavin, commander of the US 82nd Airborne, had captured his objective *and successfully maintained it* that same September during the great Montgomery attack north. And Gavin added, "There is no doubt that in our system he would have been summarily relieved and sent home in disgrace."

What Gavin did not understand was that the little beaky-nosed British Field-Marshal could not allow the Battle of Arnhem to be regarded as a failure. The 1st British Airborne Division, and the man who had commanded it, had to be regarded as heroes in an operation which he was already claiming was a "ninety-nine per cent success".

Prince Bernhard, commander-in-chief of Dutch Forces, would remark cynically when he heard of this claim, "My country can never again afford the luxury of another Montgomery success!"[21]

Ever since the Western Allies had broken out of the Normandy beachheads and raced across France into Belgium and Luxembourg, chasing the Wehrmacht in front of them, a rabble of broken disorganized units, Montgomery had been advocating one single thrust – naturally under his command – which would "bounce the Rhine" and strike for the enemy's capital, Berlin.

In the second week of September he had received Eisenhower's approval to do just that: to launch a three division airborne attack sixty miles deep into enemy-held Holland with the foremost airborne division, the 1st British, capturing the vital bridge over the Rhine. It was such a bold and uncharacteristic scheme that US General Bradley, Montgomery's bitter rival, was to comment later: "Had the pious, teetotal Montgomery wobbled into SHAEF with a hangover, I could not have been more astonished . . . Although I never reconciled myself to the venture, I nevertheless freely concede that it was one of the most imaginative of the war."[22]

But it had failed – and failed miserably. As Cyril Ray, the war correspondent who had dropped with the Americans, later said bitterly: "We tart up our reverses so heroically that it takes an effort to grasp that Arnhem was not *merely* a British defeat, but a German *victory*!"[23] Or as Captain R. W. Thompson, another war correspondent who had seen much of war, put it: "The plain fact is that the 1st Airborne had been parachuted out upon a hopeless and impossible limb in accordance with a vain and irresponsibly optimistic plan, inadequately thought out."[24]

But very few were listening to the Rays and Thompsons in the Allied camp that autumn of 1944. Montgomery rode roughshod over any criticism levelled at the first abortive attempt to take the Rhine by storm, loyally supported by Premier Winston Churchill. Now, even before the full scale of the Arnhem débâcle was assessed, he gave orders that a new plan should be formulated to attack the Rhine yet again, in a new place and with new forces. But it would be six long months before Field-Marshal Montgomery could attempt to "bounce the Rhine" again; and by then much would have changed.

TWO

It was Thanksgiving Day, 1944, when they started to move into the mountains that barred the way to the Rhine. It was a wild, stormy night with the rain slanting down in the beams from the headlights like a curtain of steel rods. For although the US Army's vehicles always drove blacked out at night, the commander of this division of General Haislip's Corps had ordered his drivers to roll with their headlights full on. It was the only way they were going to conquer the narrow winding roads of the Vosges mountains and surprise the Germans dug in on the plains beyond.

Some of them had been given a Thanksgiving Day dinner – a piece of cold turkey – just before they had set out and would eat it in the middle of the night on lonely Alsatian roads, already made treacherous by the first snows of the year. But the great majority of these soldiers setting off on their desperate journey on that last Thanksgiving Day of World War Two would have disdained turkey and cranberry sauce; their finely tuned palates would not have accepted such fare. For although they wore the olive drab of the US Army and the vehicles they drove – Shermans, jeeps, White scout cars – were American, they were not. They were the men of General Leclerc's 2nd French Armoured Division.

There were, of course, some Americans among them, for the French division belonged to US General Patch's Seventh Army. Lieutenant Tony Triumpho of the attached American artillery battalion was one of them. As they climbed ever higher into the Vosges, he was up front in a jeep with two GIs. It was the Lieutenant's task to set up a forward artillery observation post for General Leclerc, who liked to direct his own artillery fire from the front. That night as he sat hunched in the jeep, gnawing his cold leg of turkey, the rain beating a cold tattoo on the windscreen, Triumpho thought that "the plan was for the French to get just over the other side of the Vosges and then wait for the American infantry to come up for a combined attack on Strasbourg." But as he admitted ruefully after the war, "The French, of course, had another plan."[1]

Back at General Leclerc's forward command post, set up in a commandeered château in the wooded foothills of the Vosges, the air was electric with tension and anticipation. Captain Chatel, who had joined the 2nd from the Resistance, was attempting to snatch some sleep with the rest of the staff on the hard wooden floor, but without much success, for the severe-faced moustached General "kept coming in and asking if there was any news."[2] Old campaigner though he was, Leclerc was anxious and restless. It was not simply that he wanted to cross the Vosges this terrible wintry night, with the rain lashing the tall windows of the château; he wanted more. He wanted to fulfil that promise made so many years before, to take Strasbourg from the Boche – and, if his luck held out, to cross the Rhine itself.

"*Mon Général*, here I can do no more. I ask your permission to take my chance."[3] Captaine le Vicomte Philippe de Hauteclocque, son of an aristocratic French family renowned for their bravery in battle, was asking his divisional commander for formal permission to desert.

On this twenty-eighth day of May, 1940, with the heavy guns of the permanent barrage rumbling in the distance and the long pathetic columns of shabby peasant refugees heading south before the ever-victorious Wehrmacht, the thirty-seven-year-old Captain with the intense challenging blue eyes knew that the French Army was doomed. Soon it would lay down its arms. But not he. The scion of the de Hauteclocques would continue to fight against the Germans wherever he could find an opportunity to do so.

Thus it was that the Captain left his division and attempted to join the five French divisions still fighting around Lille. But by the time he reached Lille, dodging Germans all the time, the battle was over and the divisions were dispersed. Now he was on the run, a fugitive in his own country, with his fellow countrymen refusing him food and shelter, even a priest in one case, for fear the victorious Germans might shoot them. The Captain reflected bitterly that he seemed to be the only man left in the whole of France who wished to continue the fight against the Boche.

At one stage he was captured by the Germans. But he managed to talk his way out of the makeshift prisoner-of-war camp. He found a French armoured unit willing to fight and took part in one of the Army's last counter-attacks. Then he was wounded in a Stuka dive-bomber attack. When he woke up in hospital at the little town of Avallon, the war was over for France and he only just managed to escape capture for a second time.

Wounded as he was, with seemingly the hand of every Frenchman against him, he nevertheless managed to make his way south and elude the Germans. On June 17th, he heard a certain General de Gaulle broadcasting from London, repeating his call to Frenchmen to escape and join him.

"France is not alone," thundered the voice from the wireless set. "I, General de Gaulle, now in London, call on all officers and soldiers now in Britain, or who come to Britain with or without their arms to join me. ... Whatever happens, the flame of French resistance must not and will not go out!"[4]

At last Captain de Hauteclocque knew what he had to do. Six weeks later, now bearing the *nom de guerre* of Leclerc – to protect his family from any possible reprisals – he was on his way to French Africa with a mission "to rally" the French colonies there. "Your immediate objective," de Gaulle had told him in London, "is to rally French Africa. Your long-term policy is to free France!"[5,6]

Nearly one year later, Leclerc – helped by the British – had marched at the head of a motley army of white Colonial and native troops nearly three thousand miles from the French African coast, right through Chad and into the Italian colony of Libya. Here in the bakingly hot desert, much of it unknown and unmapped, they were met by two long-range desert patrols of Guards and New Zealanders, who led the French through a raging sandstorm to the remote fortified Italian outpost at Kufra, which was to be the scene of the first real Free French victory of World War Two.

The oasis at Kufra, its central feature two sapphire lakes of salt water, was a considerable place with a mosque, mud houses, market place and many fresh-water wells, all dominated by the fort of El-Taj. This fort was now going to be Colonel Leclerc's main objective.

El-Taj was the sort of fort familiar to cinema audiences of the day from many a Hollywood movie, usually associated with some desperate struggle between Tuareg tribesmen and the French Foreign

Legion. It was a great four-square fortification with very high walls of immense thickness, which Leclerc now set about attacking in true Hollywood fashion. Mobile patrols were sent out to harass the defenders while his Senegalese sharpshooters – giant black men, their faces disfigured with the ritual scars of their tribal initiations – crept up close to snipe at the Italian defenders.

By February 22nd, 1941, Leclerc's men had driven the defenders back to a few major strongpoints from which, however, they still brought down heavy artillery and machine-gun fire on the attackers as they moved in closer and closer.

Four days later when Leclerc had grown weary of the siege in that burning heat, he decided to trick the Italians into surrendering. On the night of February 26th, he ordered 250 cases of captured Italian bombs to be exploded. The result was spectacular. The Italians, having forgotten about the dump, were amazed that the French still had so much ammunition. Next morning as the French opened fire once more, and the first shell cut down the Italian flag flying proudly over what was left of the fort, the Italians asked for a truce. The Italian Commandant wanted to evacuate their wounded while there was still time.

Leclerc refused to allow a truce; he knew by now that the Italian resolve was weakening. The Italians would either surrender unconditionally or take the consequences, he told them. They made no reply. All that day and throughout the freezing cold night, Leclerc's artillery pounded the fort with what was left of its ammunition.

As dawn came on March 1st, with only a handful of shells left for his 75 mm cannon, Leclerc saw the white flag of surrender flying over El-Taj. He had beaten them!

Later that day Leclerc cabled de Gaulle in London to inform him of the first Free French victory; the Cross of Lorraine now flew over Kufra. He ended his cable thus: "We will not rest until the flag of France also flies over Paris and Strasbourg."[7]

Three years later, courtesy of the US Army, Leclerc was allowed to enter Paris, thus fulfilling the "Oath of Kufra" as it had become known in Free French circles. On August 25th, 1944, a perfect sunny summer day, Leclerc re-entered Paris after an absence of four years, at the head of a motley 2nd French Armoured Division, made up of the original Free French volunteers; regular Vichy soldiers who had come over to him after the defeat of the Germans in French North Africa;

and young men of the Resistance who were flocking to join his ranks in ever larger numbers.

But here Leclerc had run into problems. The newly formed French First Army, under General de Lattre de Tassigny, had come up from the south under the overall command of General Devers' Sixth US Army Group. Now the French wanted the only effective French armoured division to join this new First Army.

Leclerc was bitterly angry at this suggestion. "We are the original Free French," he declared. "I will not serve with any commanders who previously obeyed Vichy and who I consider to be turncoats!" So, despite all de Gaulle's threats and promises, Leclerc remained with the Americans. General Patch later reported that at their first meeting Leclerc made it "very distinctly" clear to him that "he did not want to serve with the First French Army. He did not explain why, so I decided to assign him back to General Haislip's XV Corps."[8]

In Haislip Leclerc found the ideal superior. The big American had been a student in France at the Ecole de Guerre. He spoke French fluently, understood the French mentality and was a francophile. He knew he couldn't issue orders to Leclerc like he could to another American general. "Leclerc and his men came to me," Haislip recalled later, "as representatives of the new France and had every reason to be intensely proud of what they had already done. . . . With this in mind, I never issued orders to Leclerc. . . . Whenever I wanted him to do something, I would say: 'Leclerc this is what I am planning to do. It looks to me as though you could do this and that and so forth . . . I want you to go away and study it and tell me what you think.'"[9]

So in November 1944, although officially in reserve, Leclerc started to study maps of the front in Alsace, while the infantry divisions of Haislip's Corps slogged slowly forward against stiff resistance. As one of his surbordinates, Captain Girard, later recalled: "He studied the map very closely. He searched for little entries, little narrow roads, or even tracks through which he might infiltrate his tanks. It was the same as he had done at Kufra."[10]

The map showed that there was really only one gap through which Leclerc could send armour through the Vosges and that was at the town of Saverne. But he noted, too, the little side roads on both sides of the famed Saverne Gap, a classic east–west invasion route. He made his decision; he would send four or five columns up to the mountains on those little side roads. In Captain Girard's words: "He was determined to take Strasbourg, completely by surprise and undamaged."

General Leclerc was intent upon redeeming his promise back in 1941. He had taken Paris already, now he would take Strasbourg too. Then came the Rhine...

So thus the General waited as his columns crept ever deeper through the Vosges mountains, shrouded in darkness and torrential rain. War correspondent Price Day, who was with them, reported home to his paper: "Rain and snow are the rule in this part of France but today's rain deserves special mention. It does not fall from the clouds; it is dumped as if from a bottomless bucket. It descends the hillsides in white, boiling sheets, going fast to seek low ground. It pours through woods in torrents where streams have never been before. It turns two-foot brooks into 100-yard rivers charging through valleys. Every space of low ground is a lake and the larger lakes have woods, farms and houses sitting in the middle of them..."[11]

The hours ticked by in heavy brooding tension in Leclerc's château HQ as he waited for news – news that one of his columns had outwitted the Germans and reached the other side of the Vosges, from whence he would launch the second stage of his bold, completely unauthorized plan.

It came just before dawn. One of his têtes brûlées ("burned heads") as the veterans of Africa were called in the French Army, a swarthy-faced Major who had served with Leclerc at Kufra, brought word that Major Massu's column had reached Dabo, the first little town on the other side of the Vosges.

Leaping into action, Leclerc ordered Captain Chatel to Haislip's HQ. "Tell him immediately," Leclerc snapped, eyes flashing in spite of his sleepless night, "I need one or two battalions of American infantry to clean up alongside the roads behind us and deal with all the prisoners. We don't want to be bothered waiting about to take prisoners. Bring me those battalions yourself, Captain!"[12]

The young French Captain set off through the rain-swept dawn, knowing that Haislip was too shrewd not to guess what Leclerc was up to now. Where was Leclerc going to in such haste, Haislip would reason, that he needed American infantry to mop up German prisoners and pockets of resistance left behind the tanks? It was obvious. Leclerc was not going to stop Massu on the other side of the mountains; he was pushing on!

Haislip was awakened from a deep sleep by the arrival of the young officer with his urgent request from his divisonal commander, but as Chatel recalled after the war, "he was very nice about it".

At first Haislip refused to give the French the necessary infantry "because the armour had a bad habit of trying to borrow soldiers from infantry divisions to save getting their own infantry chewed up". But gradually he weakened; he told Chatel he could have an infantry battalion from the US 79th Infantry Divison. Chatel breathed an inner sigh of relief. Obviously the francophile Corps Commander was not going to stand in Leclerc's way. It was just about then that Haislip was called to the phone. It was Patch, the US Seventh Army Commander.

To Chatel, who understood English, it was "evident that Patch was forbidding any dash for Strasbourg by Leclerc". Then he heard Haislip say: "Sir, we cannot take 'no' completely for an answer. Will you please confirm that it can be done?"[14]

A great argument followed, while Chatel waited on tenterhooks and the rain slashed savagely at the windows of the HQ, making the window panes rattle furiously. Time was rapidly running out. Massu's bold dash on that minor road leading through the walled village of Wasserlone and on to Strasbourg itself would soon be bogged down if he had to use what little infantry he had to tackle every Boche strongpoint on the way.

Now Chatel heard Haislip use the arguments on Patch that Leclerc had used on him. Strasbourg was not only strategically important, Haislip said, it also had great emotional meaning for the whole of the French nation. It was more than a mere objective; it was a symbol – just as Paris had been.

In the end General Patch gave in – a little. Leclerc could patrol in the general direction of Strasbourg, but only when General Haislip gave the word.

Haislip hung up and faced the tense young Frenchman. "You can do it – but only upon my order." Then he added, "General Leclerc does know, of course, that he is only supposed to take the passes of the Vosges and not go further?"

Chatel assured him that Leclerc did understand that. And with this news he set off on the return journey to the château.

Two hours later Chatel was back at Haislip's HQ. Three of Leclerc's armoured columns had already reached their objectives on the other side of the mountains. Leclerc was ready to go all out for Strasbourg. The harassed young French Captain had had just enough time to gulp down a cup of coffee before Leclerc sent him back to the Americans, to ask for permission for the 2nd Armoured Division to "patrol" in the direction of the Alsatian town. He got it. The last push was on its way.

The French moved so swiftly that the Germans in the little townships on the other side of the Vosges – Cirey, Voyer, Rehtal, Dabo and the like – were caught completely by surprise. Corporal Emil Fray, a Breton who had escaped to England and volunteered his services to General de Gaulle in person, was in one of the 30-ton Shermans slithering and lurching in the thick mud down the narrow roads. He remembered later: "German soldiers, covered with mud, slumped all along the sides of the roads. There were guns, which had been pushed into water-filled ditches, dead cattle and horses, all manner of vehicles and weapons, shot down and to pieces by us as we rushed forward. Soon, where they could, the Germans were pulling out everything they had."[15]

Wynford Vaughan Thomas, the BBC's war correspondent who was there at the time, reported to his audience back home: "They [the French] ramble over the ugly military bridges that span the swollen streams and then they climb into the hills and cold squalls of rain sweep down on them and drench them, and then the rain suddenly gives place to snow – blanketing blinding snow, or a cruel driving sleet that cuts the soldiers' faces and freezes in solid sheets on the windscreens of the trucks. The drivers drive with bare, red hands – the gloves can't grip the slippery wheel that whirls this way and that with every bump and pot-hole and everything slithering on the icy road. On they go, these endless, urgent columns crowding on every highway, debouching into the rough country tracks that are churned into seething glaciers of mud – mud surges up in an oily flood to the footboard, mud flies in a dense spray from the whirling wheels, coating men and machines as completely as paint sprayed from an air gun."[16]

Sergeant Bill Maudlin, the American cartoonist, was so impressed by the way the French drove that last week of November as they advanced on Strasbourg that he drew a cartoon for the *Stars and Stripes*, the US Army newspaper. It showed a line of disconsolate American truck drivers being addressed by their lieutenant before departure. "Men," says the officer gravely, "some of you may never come back. *There's a French convoy on the road!*"

The French Shermans rumbled into Phalsbourg and raced on under terrible conditions to Saverne, a typical Alsatian town ringed by vineyards, and the organizational centre of the Vosges defences. The German staff of General Bruhn, the Regional Commander, were caught completely unawares. The whole of the German HQ, including the flabbergasted General, were captured, the elegant staff officers staring in horror at these tough mud-spattered Frenchmen in American uniform who had appeared out of nowhere.

So great was the surprise that day that the French were able to set up an ambush on the road leading from the town to Strasbourg; for the Germans, still not realizing that Saverne had fallen into French hands, were sending up reinforcements for the Vosges front. Corporal Fray recalls how they positioned their tanks between the houses on either side of the road through a village and lay in wait for the Germans: "It was an absolute massacre. We just let them come as close as possible and then shot them to bits – there were all sorts, lorried infantry, guns, trucks, staff cars, even the German Chief of Railways for the region, who was in a camouflaged Citroen. With guns and machine guns we poured fire into them until the roads were absolutely littered with burning vehicles."[17]

Now Leclerc tried one of the tricks he'd learnt from his old chief General Patton. Sometimes, when he had been taking things into his own hands by disobeying an order or misinterpreting it to his own advantage, Patton was wont to disappear to the front, deliberately out of touch with his HQ. On the second day of the drive for Strasbourg, Leclerc did the same. He came up to Saverne. He told Chatel: "You stay close to me. I don't want you to go back to Corps HQ, because I don't want you to bring me any counter-orders."[18] And he stationed staff officers along key roads leading to Saverne, with instructions to head off any American emissary bringing orders to stop him driving for the Rhenish city.

Indeed one such officer was already on his way – General Menoher, Haislip's Chief-of-Staff, who was bearing a direct command from Eisenhower himself not to head for Strasbourg. But Leclerc's ploy worked. By the time Menoher did reach Leclerc, Strasbourg had already been taken.

At dawn on the morning of November 23rd, Leclerc gave the order to drive for the city. They were to take Strasbourg by surprise, for it had a strong garrison of 15,000 men; and Leclerc was realist enough to know that not all Alsatians welcomed the return of the French. Any of the German-speaking locals might betray the advance to the garrison if they got wind of it. The 2nd Armoured Divison would have to make the swiftest advance of its combat career if it were to succeed.

Englishman Dennis Wood, a Quaker with the Red Cross, who would one day win the *Croix de Guerre* for bravery under fire, was up with the leading column in his ambulance. He reported later, "We saw the German troops streaming out towards Saverne. They hadn't the faintest idea of what was happening and went straight into the trap."[19]

Lieutenant Tony Triumpho was one of the three Americans to go in with the French that day. "We ... went roaring across the plain in our jeep along with four or five light tanks and a few half tracks of infantry, altogether about 70 men. We passed working parties and groups of German troops ... and they just stood open-mouthed. When they saw it was French troops they were scared to death, for they had heard that the French ... did not take too many prisoners."[20]

But the French were too intent on capturing Strasbourg to waste time shooting prisoners. Every minute counted now, as the Shermans in the lead lumbered down the flat roads of the plain, trying to catch the first glimpse of that church on the horizon that would indicate they were almost there – the towers of Strasbourg Cathedral.

Corporal Fray was one of those at the point. "We hardly met any opposition," he recalled later, "because we were going so fast the enemy never had a chance to establish positions in front of us."[21]

At ten thirty that morning the French burst into Strasbourg, guns blazing. There might not have been many of them but they sounded like an entire army as their tracked vehicles rattled over the wet glistening *pavé*, and the first citizens ran out of their high, half-timbered houses to greet the liberators exuberantly. They didn't linger. They had been ordered to bypass the outlying forts and head for the Pont de Kehl, the supreme objective, the bridge across the Rhine at Kehl.

The first column, led by Major Rouvillois, barrelled through the narrow twisting streets of the city, firing to left and right like drunken cowboys shooting up some Wild West settlement in a Hollywood film. Many a German military window-shopper was caught by surprise, and went dropping for cover as machine-gunfire ripped the store windows apart. Then, within six hundred yards of their objective, their wild dash came to an abrupt halt as the German guns thundered from the other side of the Rhine. The Shermans scuttled for cover, blindly seeking shelter from the 88 mm shells coming howling down.

Major Massu, who would one day achieve notoriety as the leader of the "paras revolt" in North Africa, was stopped momentarily by the German defenders of Fort Foch. But, with the bold decisiveness that marked his whole career, he switched routes immediately. Now he followed the path taken by Rouvillois' column, ignoring the baleful shrieks of the 88 mms and the slugs pattering against the metal sides of his halftrack like tropical rain on a tin roof.

Behind him more and more French vehicles headed for that vital bridge, watched by German officers and their ladies of the garrison who sat transfixed in the cafés, coffee cups half-raised to their lips, or stood paralysed at bus stops with the customary briefcase in hand, waiting to be transported to offices already under siege by the French.

Vaughan Thomas, who was close behind the leading columns racing for the bridge, had just passed the cathedral "with its great spire ... soaring up over the medieval house-tops" when he saw it: "set against the rain-dark sky to the east, a looming outline of the distant hills – the Black Forest, the western barrier of Hitler's Reich, Germany. We felt as if we'd come to the end of a long journey ... *We'd got to the Rhine at last!*"[22]

Leclerc arrived in the city just around that time, and drove straight to the Hotel Kaiserpalast, the German HQ. Here he accepted the surrender of the German commander and some nine thousand soldiers and proceeded to drink the cups of coffee, still hot, which the German staff had just had made for themselves. He and his staff were still standing around excitedly discussing events and drinking the captured *café* when Colonel Dio, who had been with him right from the start in Africa, swaggered in.

Leclerc, in high good humour, greeted his comrade of the Kufra days with a slap on the back. "*Hein, mon vieux Dio!*" he chortled. "So here we are. Now at least the two of us can drop dead!"[23]

At that very moment, with a roar like an express train passing through a station at top speed, three German shells slammed into the hotel. A gigantic crystal chandelier from the ballroom ceiling hurtled to the ground. Outside on the grand stairway, three or four soldiers were flung about like rag dolls. The air was filled with smoke and the acrid stink of high explosive.

Even before the dust had settled Leclerc was doubled up with mirth, laughing like crazy at the macabre thought that in the very same instant he had told his old comrade he could drop dead, it had almost happened. All the same, in spite of his laughter, Leclerc knew the Germans were too close for comfort. Not only were they still holding out inside the city, particularly in the forts which ringed the place, but they were also readying themselves on the eastern bank of the Rhine for what they obviously expected was to come: a thrust across the bridge at Kehl.

The steam had gone out of the French drive for the Rhine. Not one of the many bridges which crossed the waterways leading up to the Rhine itself had yet been blown, and the great road bridge at Kehl over the river was still intact. The French had rushed the city too swiftly for the German engineers to have detonated their explosive charges, but it wouldn't be long before they did so, wherever they could, and now the defenders' fire was growing in intensity.

Vaughan Thomas, following up the advance, noted that to get to the Kehl bridge one passed through "an industrial suburb, past canals and warehouses and a station, but it's as much as your life is worth today to put your head out of a doorway and try and see the other bank. The Germans are there all right on their side. They shoot at everything that moves. They have the bridge approaches swept with small arms fire and when we left our guns were racing towards the Rhine bank to deal with them." And he concluded before signing off, "Tomorrow will decide if the French or the Germans are going to win the battle for the bridge."[24]

Those guns racing up to the Rhine were those of the US 250 Field Artillery Battalion. At two o'clock on that chaotic afternoon, the American gunners unlimbered their 105 mm cannon and opened up, pouring interdictory fire into Germany at the crossroads west of Kehl. Later the American gunners boasted they had fired the first shells into Germany in World War Two; indeed, many kept the shell-cases as souvenirs. They were wrong, however. It was men of the First Army who had fired the first shells into the Third Reich, south of Aachen, over a month before.

Lieutenant Tony Triumpho, who was one of those who kept a

shell-case as a souvenir, now decided to live up to his surname. He resolved to cross the Rhine on the Kehl land bridge and demonstrate the Allied triumph over the Germans. Together with two companions he raced across the bridge into Germany.[25] "There seemed to be nobody about," he recalled much later. "We made a reconnaissance to find out what we could and all we heard there was the chirping of the birds. It was all most eerie and deserted."[26]

Too eerie for the young artillery officer. He turned and ran back across the bridge – and it was fortunate for him that he did so, though he maintained years later that "I had the feeling that if there had been enough troops up when we went in, we could have established a bridgehead over the Rhine."

Seconds later, as he and his two companions arrived back on the French side, there was a shattering explosion. The bridge trembled and swayed like a live thing. Crackling blue and red sparks ran the whole of its length. Spurts of dust rose everywhere. Then with one final dramatic roar, a rending of tortured metal, a slither of falling masonry, the Kehl land bridge slammed into the water.

The second attempt to cross the Rhine had failed.

THREE

The day after the Germans had blown the bridge at Strasbourg, veteran war correspondent Captain R. V. Thompson visited the Rhenish city. It was a thrill for him "to stand looking out over the broad Rhine deep into Germany; to watch civilians, here a cyclist, a farm cart, going about their business in this land that had brought such misery upon the world and so terrible a retribution upon itself." And he went on:

"There is something magic, unreal, profoundly moving to look into this country, over the Rhine port of Kehl, with the smoke of its burning buildings rising lazily into the still air of this mild day: to look over the broad highways and villages to the dark line of the Black Forest, lightened now with the faint gleam of snow."[1]

But that peaceful vista was deceiving and Thompson knew it. On the other side of the great steel structure of the railway bridge now lying in crumpled ruins in the brown water of the Rhine, there ran a line of grey concrete pillboxes: part of the Siegfried Line running right along Germany's frontier with France, Luxembourg, Belgium and Holland like the backbone of some fossilized primeval monster. The enemy was still there. "There are thousands of eyes keeping watch on the Rhine," he wrote later for his readers back home, who would read his report over their meagre wartime Sunday lunch, "thousands of Germans eyes . . . It has the feel of the last barrier, and I know that when the Allied armies cross this brown river, it will be the end of Nazi Germany."[2]

Presently a shell came whizzing through the wall of the building in which Thompson was standing; as the smoke of the explosion drifted away and another struck a tree near by, he knew it was time for him to go. He had been spotted from the other side of the Rhine, it would be dangerous to linger here any longer: "I took a long last look at the Rhine, strangely peaceful in a moment of lull, and was inspired by the sight. I knew that this picture of Kehl across the river; the enemy pillboxes, half under the floods; the wreckage of the bridges; the wide plain with its fields and farms to the dark line of the Black Forest would remain with me always. There was nothing particularly dramatic about it and nothing exciting. It was because, at that moment, I knew that the enemy watch on the Rhine is utterly without hope!"[3]

But it was another four months before Captain Thomas would see the Rhine again, when Montgomery made his second attempt to cross the great river — another four months of savage combat, bloodshed and human misery. For in the next four months, the Germans would not only defend their frontiers and the river with fanatically stubborn determination, but they would also go over to the offensive again in the Ardennes and send the Allies reeling back with severe losses. Now both flanks of the Allied armies touched the Rhine. In the north, General Crerar's Canadians held the lower reaches of the river in Holland; in the south, General de Lattre de Tassigny's French held it for an area below Strasbourg. But both the French and the Canadians had other problems to concern them than the crossing of the Rhine. Indeed, they would be the last ones to cross. It would be Montgomery's armies and Bradley's in the centre who finally made the crossing — but not for four long months yet.

Even before the invasion of Europe in 1944, Allied planners had considered how to tackle the Rhine. They had envisaged two major thrusts across the river into the heart of Germany with Berlin as the ultimate objective.

One thrust was to pass north of the Ardennes and aim at the Ruhr industrial area. The Ruhr is shaped like a triangle with one side running along the Rhine from Cologne to Duisburg. Being thickly populated, with one city virtually merging into another everywhere, the Ruhr would obviously be an area to be avoided. It would swallow up troops too quickly and greedily. Therefore the other thrust, passing south of the Ardennes, would again skirt the Ruhr. When both of these drives had successfully crossed the Rhine, they would link up north of the Ruhr and encircle it, thus isolating the great factories, such as Krupp's, which supplied the Wehrmacht with its weapons.

Thereafter, while the Ruhr was left to rot on the vine, one powerful main drive would thrust across the North German plain for Berlin, while a secondary force would head north-eastwards from Frankfurt towards Kassel. This, then, had been the plan back in 1944, when the British had been the senior partners in the Anglo-American alliance and the Americans were the "Johnnies-Come-Lately", as they called themselves.

But that December, when Leclerc – now considered a downright hindrance to Franco-American co-operation and goodwill – was transferred to what was virtually a non-combatant assignment a hundred miles from the front on the Rhine, things had begun to change. After what the Americans regarded as the débâcles of Caen and Arnhem, Montgomery's star was beginning to fade; they accused him of being too slow, too set in his ways, and, more importantly, of trying to hog all the glory for himself and Britain, despite the fact that American soldiers now outnumbered the British by three to one.

The final decisive change in the Anglo-American partnership occurred later that month. Following the German assault on American forces in the Ardennes on December 16th, 1944, taking General Bradley completely by surprise, Eisenhower gave Montgomery command of the two northernmost US armies, the First and the Ninth. The British Field-Marshal was thus commanding more American troops than General Bradley himself – and when this news was released on January 5th, 1945, there was a storm of protest.

As Colonel Hansen, one of Bradley's staff, recorded at time: "The effect has been a cataclysmic Roman Holiday in the British press, which has exulted over the announcement and hailed it as an increase in Montgomery's command." Bitterly Hansen went on, "Many of us who were avowed Anglophiles in Great Britain have now been irritated, hurt and infuriated by the British radio and press. All this good feeling has vanished under these circumstances until today we regard the people we once looked upon as warm and sympathetic friends, as people whom we must instead distrust for fear of being hoodwinked ... Their press is building a well of resentment among our American troops that can be never emptied, a distrust that cannot be erased."[4]

Two days later, Montgomery – who claimed in his memoirs to be perturbed "about the sniping at Eisenhower which was going on in the British press" – held a press conference "to put in a strong plea for Allied solidarity". His intentions may have been good, but the effect was simply to add fuel to the fire. His condescending words gave the impression that he was St George come to slay the dragon, that he alone could lead the Americans to victory. Even his own Chief-of-Staff, General Freddie de Guingand, described his tone as "What a good boy am I!"

Colonel Hansen and Colonel Ralph Ingersoll, founder of the New York newspaper *PM*, and no friend of Britain in the first place, exploded with rage. Both of them went to Bradley and told him he had to make a stand. Bradley, as Ingersoll recorded just after the war, "for the first, last and only time in the campaign, got all-out right-down-to-his-toes mad!" And in the heat of the moment he telephoned Eisenhower, told him about the Montgomery press conference, and stated categorically: "After what has happened, I cannot serve under Montgomery. If he is to be put in command of all ground forces, you must send me home, for if Montgomery goes in over me, I will have lost the confidence of my command ... This is one thing I cannot take."[5] He added that Patton, his best commander, had assured him that he would not serve under Montgomery either.

Eisenhower by now was well aware of the resentment that his generals felt towards the British Field-Marshal, and realized the situation could not be allowed to continue. So, trying to soothe Bradley's ruffled feelings, he removed the US First Army from under Montgomery's command. But Montgomery still retained the US Ninth Army, and as January gave way to February and the Allied forces advanced ever closer to the Rhine, the thorny question arose once more; who would deliver the major attack?

Exhausted as the Germans were, they were still highly dangerous. That month, the British troops fighting in the Reichswald to clear the way to the Rhine were taking *one thousand dead a day*, and double that number in wounded. Thus the British Chiefs-of-Staff suggested to Eisenhower that he did not have sufficient strength to make two major thrusts across the Rhine as had been planned back in 1944; instead they recommended he should make only one major attack across the Rhine – in the north. This would be closer to the Allies' chief supply port at Antwerp; it would provide a more direct menace to the Ruhr; and it would get the troops more quickly onto the North German plain and the road to Berlin, "the glittering prize" as Eisenhower himself called it. There was only one drawback. The general who commanded in the north was none other than Montgomery. Was the detested little Field-Marshal going to receive the kudos of final victory?

Thus when Bradley was ordered on February 1st, 1945, to stop Patton's offensive into the Moselle-Saar region and remove some of his infantry divisions to bolster up the strength of Simpson's Ninth Army (which was under Montgomery's command), the trouble commenced yet once more.

That day Bradley called Patton at his CP. "Monty did it again, George," he announced. "You and Hodges [commander of the First US Army] will go on the defensive while Montgomery will resume the offensive in the north." Anticipating Patton's explosive reaction, he added hastily: "It wasn't Ike this time. Orders from the Combined Chiefs. Brooke [head of the British Imperial Staff] even got General Marshall to go along with him. I don't know what made him agree. Probably he's anxious to get those fourteen British divisions sitting on their butts in Belgium back into action."

"What are they hoping to accomplish?" Patton spluttered.

"Montgomery wants to secure a wide stretch of the Rhine as quickly as possible," Bradley replied.

"Horseshit!" Patton snorted angrily. "I'm convinced that we have a much better chance to get to the Rhine first with our present attack."[6]

An idea had been born ...

A little later Patton attended Bradley's Army Group conference at his headquarters in Namur to listen to the full version of the plan. Patton was in a good mood, despite the bad news. He told his fellow generals one of his many anti-Montgomery stories. "The Field-Marshal was outlining his plans to Eisenhower," he said with a mean grin on his long face, "and concluded as follows: 'I shall dispose several divisions on my flank and lie in wait for the Hun. Then at the proper moment I shall leap on him' – Patton paused dramatically for the punchline – '*like a savage rabbit!*'"[7]

The assembled generals laughed dutifully and then Patton became serious. Announcing the transfer of the American divisions to Montgomery's command, he commented: "It is very obvious now who is running this war over here and how it is being run." But Patton had already made up his mind that he was going to disobey the ruling from the top. "Personally," he said in that high-pitched voice of his, which seemed so strange in such a masculine man, "I think that it would be a foolish and ignoble way for the Americans to end the war by sitting on our butts. And, gentlemen, we aren't going to do anything foolish or ignoble." Thereupon he announced that he would continue his attack towards the Rhine – but he counselled the strictest secrecy. "Let the gentlemen up north learn what we are doing," he said sombrely, "when they see it on their maps."[8]

So, while Montgomery up north continued his ponderous preparations for a set-piece attack on the Rhine, Patton was quietly planning to beat him to it. And Patton was not the only one to ignore official strategy. As Colonel Ingersoll recorded: "After the Ardennes no one was ever frank with anyone. Fair, there was a scrupulous effort to be – almost a doubling over backwards; but frank, never. Bradley – and Patton, Hodges and Simpson under Bradley's direction – proceeded to make and carry out their plans without the assistance of official command channels, on a new basis, openly discussed among themselves. This squarely faced the facts that in order to defeat the enemy, by direct attack and in the shortest possible time, they had (1) to conceal their plans from the British, and (2) to almost literally outwit Eisenhower's Supreme Headquarters, half of which was British and the other half of which was beyond their power to influence by argument. They completely succeeded in both objectives and won the war."[9]

A cynic might have commented: "And in addition *lost the peace*." For what was going to happen on the Rhine now would shift the whole balance of Allied strategy to the south of Germany, involve the US Army in a purposeless fight that consumed at least eighteen divisions in house-to-house fighting in the Ruhr, and left the Allied armies too weak to make that last dash for the "glittering prize". In the end the Russians would claim that prize, just as they would claim Prague and Vienna. Berlin would be left to the Red Army, and the whole structure and fate of post-war Central Europe would be changed . . .

FOUR

On the night of March 2nd, 1945, as the guns rumbled in the distance and the sky glowed orange with the persistent explosion of heavy shells, the first attempt was made to seize a bridge across the Rhine since Leclerc's men had dashed across the bridge at Kehl four months before.

Scouts from the leading elements of General Simpson's Ninth Army had reported that there were two bridges still standing across the Rhine to north and south of the great Ruhr city of Dusseldorf: at Oberkassel and Uerdingen. To Simpson, tall, skinny and known to the US Regular Army as "Big Simp", they were a tempting but potentially disastrous objective. The area around Dusseldorf was a densely built up industrial area in which his Ninth Army might well bog down, fighting for every factory, railhead and rolling mill. But Simpson was not very happy with the small role which Montgomery had assigned to his Ninth in the great set-piece crossing of the Rhine. He saw here a chance to get across first and create a bigger role for the men under his command.

Now a composite force of the 736th Tank Battalion, the 643rd Tank Destroyer Battalion, and riflemen of the 83rd Division's 330th Infantry prepared a Trojan Horse operation, which they hoped would take them through the German lines and enable them to snatch the vital bridge from right under the German defenders' noses.

The riflemen, specially chosen for their fluency in the German language, were dressed up in captured German uniforms and steel helmets and formed into an advance platoon which would ride with the tanks at the point. Unfortunately the task force did not possess captured German armour, so they were forced to compromise: they would disguise their American tanks to look like German ones – at least, they hoped that in the darkness the German defenders would take them for that. Since the American M4 tank lacked the typical German muzzle brakes on its cannon, the Americans taped cut-down ammunition tubes to the end of the Shermans' guns. The white star insignia on the turret was hidden by a coat of green paint and large white identification numbers were added, as customary on German tanks. Finally the "buggy-whip" radio aerials were tied down, as they were much more prominent than the German rod aerials.

As soon as darkness fell they moved out, pushing forward towards the enemy lines in columns of threes in the German fashion. They swung onto the main road leading to Oberkassel. The order was given: no talking, no smoking. The men complied without question. Everyone knew they ran the risk of being shot for wearing the enemy's uniform if they were captured. They were taking no risks.

They passed the first German outposts. No one attempted to stop them. A column of German infantry marched up. Obediently they moved to one side to let the tanks rumble by. Everything was going smoothly. They reached Oberkassel, well behind German lines, without a single shot being fired. The vital bridge was within reach...

As the first light of dawn began to flush the sky to the east, a German soldier on a bicycle appeared out of nowhere and scanned the column with obvious suspicion. Suddenly he started to pedal all out, body bent low over the handlebars.

"*He's spotted us!*" someone shouted excitedly.

One of the Americans flung up his rifle, aimed and fired in the same instant. The bicycle came to a sudden stop and the German toppled off, dead before he hit the tarmac.

Abruptly the air-raid sirens began to sound a shrill warning. At top speed the column raced for the city, angry scarlet flame stabbing the dawn gloom on all sides, tracer winging lethally back and forth. Now they were in the place itself, dashing through the bomb-shattered streets, heading for the bridge.

The lead tank swung round a corner. There it was – the bridge! The commander urged his driver forward. Too late. German engineers were running for their lives. A series of angry blue sparks ran the length of the bridge. The girders trembled. There was an angry rumbling sound. Suddenly the centre of the bridge exploded in a ball of red and yellow flame. A huge mushroom of smoke raced for the sky. What was left of the bridge slithered and splashed into the Rhine.

Once again, the Allies had failed.

Now it was the turn of the "Hell of Wheels", the famed 2nd Armored Division, which had once been commanded by no less a person than "Blood and Guts" Patton himself. Renowned for its dash and daring, so far in the long campaign in Europe the 2nd Armored had never once given up any ground that it had conquered. Together with infantry attached from the US 95th Infantry Division, the tankers of the 2nd Armored had orders to capture the huge, three-span *Adolf Hitler Brücke*, stretching 1,640 feet across the Rhine at Uerdingen.

This time there would be no subterfuge employed. It would be a straightforward armoured dash to snatch the bridge from the defenders – a bold *coup de main* in true Patton fashion. The capture of the bridge bearing the Führer's own name would be, as one of the attackers recalled later, "a smack in the eye for Adolf". Unfortunately for the Americans, however, Adolf never did receive that particular punch in his optic.

It was only a few hours since Colonel Sidney Hinds of the 2nd Armored's most forward group had heard that he had been selected for the mission. General White, his divisional commander, had called him on the radio on the night of March 1st and given him his instructions in clear.

"Want someone to throw a rock into that big ditch," White said, trying to confuse any German picking up his call. "It is very important."

Hinds realized he meant the Rhine. "We will be close enough before daylight," he replied.

"Let us know as soon as you do," White answered. "It will be quite a newsbreak for us. Understand?"

Hinds understood. As always the old "Hell on Wheels" was eager for publicity back home. "Will it be necessary to throw a rock into it?" he asked.

"You can have someone peter-easy-easy in it. It will be OK," White said. Thus, cryptically, White was one of the first to suggest something that would become almost a tradition over the next few weeks, with everyone from Patton to Churchill doing it: namely, urinate into the Rhine.

"OK," Hinds replied with a grin before signing off, "I'll peter-easy-easy in it myself!"

Many years later Hinds recalled with a twinkle in his eye: "*And I did!*"[1]

The attack commenced at 12.30 on the afternoon of March 2nd. Tankers and infantry fought their way into the villages fringing the road to the river, meeting unexpectedly stiff opposition. For unknown to the Americans, the commander of the German Parachute Army holding that sector, General Schlemm, had ordered up four battalions of the German 2nd Parachute Division into the area; and the "green devils" as they called themselves were some of the best soldiers left in the Wehrmacht.

Within minutes the first four American tanks were knocked out, effectively blocking further progress. Infantry were sent to clean up the opposition. Pfc Raymond Richardson, a medic, went up with them to aid the tankers who had been wounded. Just as he was starting to bandage up the first injured man, "two bearded characters in grey-green uniforms" appeared at his side, "both of whom had pistols in their belts".[2] Thinking that they wanted to surrender, Richardson reached for their pistols – and suddenly found his arm seized in a vicious grip. The Germans did not want to surrender; they just wanted to help. Together they helped Richardson to carry the wounded to the waiting ambulance. Then they drew their weapons again and resumed the battle...

But in spite of the stiff German resistance, the men of the "Hell on Wheels" were optimistic that the Adolf Hitler Bridge would still be intact and that they could capture it. Why else would the Germans fight so fiercely, if the bridge were already blown to their rear?

At four o'clock General White ordered the divisional artillery to lay down harassing fire on the bridge area to prevent German engineers from placing demolition charges. Every thirty second they were to drop a round on both ends of the structure; he would personally take responsibility for any over-expenditure of ammunition.

Back at headquarters, as the force pushed forward steadily and night began to fall, the brass requested a paradrop on Mundelheim on the eastern bank of the river, and also asked for a company of DUKW amphibious trucks so that they could launch "an instantaneous sneak amphibious attack" before the defenders realized what was happening. But both requests were turned down. The disappointed Americans blamed this on Montgomery because, as the divisonal history of the 2nd stated later, "a first crossing by forces other than his own would rob him [Montgomery] of glory and prestige."

Whatever the reason, this was the first sign that the race to be first to cross the Rhine had become more a matter of prestige than a military necessity.

All that night the combat troops – concerned not with prestige but only with preserving their young lives – fought against "fine, young Dutch SS men", as Colonel Hinds called them, who battled tenaciously but ultimately were unable to stop the Americans. By five in the morning they had cleared the way to the bridge's approaches.

Lieutenant Peter Kostow and his section of tanks were the first to reach the bridge. Hurriedly Kostow sprang from the turret of his Sherman and, before the Germans could fire, pelted across to the other side. It was a historic moment. An American had crossed the Rhine in combat! But the young officer had no thoughts for history. Knowing now that the bridge was intact, his sole concern was to get back with the news – and a whole skin.

True, the bridge was still standing, but the German defenders were nevertheless determined to fight off the "Amis", as they called the Americans, until their engineers could blow it up. Hinds sent up two battalions of infantry with orders to capture and hold both ends of the bridge, so that US engineers could clear the structure of demolition charges. The infantrymen surged forward about a hundred yards and were actually over the Rhine when they discovered the roadbed was impassable for tanks. That did it. The infantry had no heart for combat on the other side of the Rhine without the support of tanks. They turned and pelted back for the western bank, and began to dig in.

They were still digging in when the bridge was rocked by an explosion. The night was split by a vivid burst of flame. In the glowing lurid light, the startled American infantrymen could see the huge metal structure heaving and shaking like an injured beast. Then all was dark once more and they were left there, spades in hands, blinking their eyes, trying to peer through the gloom, one question uppermost in their minds. *Had the Krauts blown the bridge?*

It was decided to send a thirteen-man volunteer patrol across, under the command of Lieutenant Miller of the 41st Infantry Regiment. Well strung out, weapons at the ready, the GIs advanced through the darkness, nerves jangling electrically, wondering if the

Germans would be waiting for them out there on the bridge. They circled a huge hole in the middle of the bridge road successfully. No sign of the Krauts. They pressed on. Now they were above the Rhine; the water was a long, long way below. If they were caught here and the bridge was blown they wouldn't have a chance; laden down with their packs and helmets they would go down like bricks. Now they reached the other side, hearts thumping wildly, hands holding their weapons damp with sweat. Lieutenant Miller hesitated. What should he do next? To his right the road was still burning. To his left, all was darkness.

Suddenly a machine gun opened up from a nearby house. Tracer bullets zipped over their heads. The startled Americans froze for an instant, then turned and ran. They had seen all they wanted to see. The bridge was still intact.

Just as they reached the other side, the bridge was shaken by a second tremendous explosion. *Had the Germans blown the damned thing after all?*

Now Captain Youngblood of the 17th Engineer Battalion advanced onto the bridge. He and his men started to cut every wire they could find, all of them knowing as they crept from wire to wire that they could be blown to smithereens at any moment. Some of them swung down over the side of the bridge, hanging out above the murky brown waters of the river, inspecting joints and suspension members for hidden demolition charges. Finally, tense and greased with sweat, they reached the other side, saw the burning tar road, and decided they had done enough: they would return to their own lines. As far as they were concerned the bridge was intact and cleared of all explosive devices.

As dawn approached, Hinds sent one of his staff officers to confer with General White. White had lost his initial enthusiasm for the project. The publicity value of capturing the first bridge across the Rhine for the "Hell on Wheels" Division no longer seemed so important to him. He didn't want to "sacrifice anything in vain". However, as Hinds was on the scene and he wasn't, White took the easy option and left the decision up to the Colonel. Whether or not Hinds decided to capture the bridge and cross the Rhine, White told the staff officer, he would back him "to the limit".

But time was finally running out on the *Adolf Hitler Brücke*.

While the Americans were conferring the Germans had crept back onto the bridge and worked feverishly to replace the severed demolition wires. Even as the Americans started to organize an all-out dawn attack on the bridge, there was a huge, ear-splitting explosion. A moment later it was followed by another – and another. On the western bank, the infantrymen preparing for the attack stood in open-mouthed awe, the blast buffeting their faces like a blow from a flabby fist, as the eastern half of the great bridge swayed and trembled, dust and smoke spiralling into the sky, then thundered into the Rhine.

Simpson's hopes of obtaining a bridge over the Rhine and beating Montgomery across were extinct. There was not a single Rhine bridge left standing in his Ninth Army's sector. Now he would have to wait until the little Britisher let him cross.

Next it was the turn of General Hodges' First US Army. Courtney Hodges, an infantryman by training, was generally regarded in the US Army as slow, methodical and plodding. Patton, the ex-cavalryman, had little respect for him, especially after Hodges' poor performance in the Battle of the Bulge in December, when he'd had to abandon his headquarters and fly for his life as enemy tanks closed on his HQ at Spa in Belgium. But Hodges did have one of the most dashing corps commanders in the whole of the Army, General "Lightning Joe" Collins, commanding his VII Corps.

That March Hodges gave Collins free rein and Collins seized the opportunity gratefully. He ordered his 104th Infantry and 3rd Armored Divisons to drive all out for the most important Rhenish city of all – Cologne. There, according to air intelligence, there was at least one bridge standing – and "Lightning Joe" intended to capture one of them.

Defending the city with two weak divisions was General Koechling, commander of LXXXI Corps, an old opponent of Collins from the previous autumn when the two of them had battled for the "Holy City" of Aachen, the first German city captured for the Allies. Now Koechling tried desperately to hang on to the Third Reich's fourth largest city. He mobilized anyone who could hold and fire a rifle – policemen, firemen, boys of the Hitler Youth – and used them to defend what was called the "inner ring" around the city, while his regular units, what was left of them, tried to hold up the Americans outside the bomb-shattered city.

Collins flung in his 3rd Armored Division, under its commander General Maurice Rose, who had exactly one more month to live before he would die in an ambush on the other side of the Rhine. Rose, a hard, feared commander, who as a Jew had made the remarkable achievement of rising from private to general in the frankly anti-semitic pre-war US Army, pushed forward relentlessly, driving his troops as hard as they would go.

From his command post in a semi-ruined brewery, Koechling watched in growing despair as his tanks of the decimated 9th Panzer Divison were knocked out one by one by the tankers of Rose's 3rd. Finally the Corps Commander was forced to make a run for it under fire.

By the early afternoon of the first day of Collins' attack, Koechling had retreated all the way into Cologne itself. His new command post was in a bunker, one kilometre from Cologne's famous landmark, the Hohenzollern Bridge, adorned by the great equestrian statue of-Queen Victoria's grandson, Kaiser Wilhelm II. The centre of Cologne was in ruins; virtually every building was shattered and gutted as a result of the world's first 1,000-bomber raid, in 1942, directed by "Bomber" Harris of the RAF. But the bridge was still intact. And, miraculous as it seemed, Cologne's cathedral, which had taken seven hundred years to build, was still standing too; for Collins had given strict instructions that its twin towers should not be used for regis-tration fire by his corps artillery.

The former city commandant was almost at the end of his tether. He told Koechling that all he had left to defend the city centre and the vital bridge was a handful of old men and boys, hastily drafted into the German home guard, the *Volkssturm*. Even as the harassed soldier related this to Koechling, the local Gauleiter came bustling into the command post, crying: "Cologne must be defended to the end! The *Volkssturm* can stop the Ami tanks with *panzerfausts!*"[3,4]

The weary staff officers watched in amazement as the "golden pheasant" – as Party officials were contemptuously called because of their love for gold braid and fancy uniforms – went from one officer to another, pleading, demanding, threatening. In the end he went out, promising that he would personally dispatch 1,200 *Volkssturm* men to Koechling to help defend Cologne. But of the Gauleiter's promised 1,200, only sixty turned up.

The last remaining tanks of the 9th Panzer Division were fighting it out with Rose's 3rd Armored Division at the city's airport. Here the desperate Germans turned their anti-aircraft guns on the Americans, using the fearsome 88 mm cannon with long overhanging muzzles in an unaccustomed ground role. For a while the Americans were stalled. Then the leading combat group put down a smokescreen and charged the German guns in true cavalry fashion, the Shermans going all out, their guns barking to left and right. After all, Rose was another of Patton's pupils, familar with his motto of "*L'audace, l'audace, toujours l'audace!*" The Germans fled – and then the whole defensive system collapsed when the commander of the 9th Panzer, the aristocratic General Freiherr von Elverfeldt, was killed in action.

On the morning of March 6th, two days after the *Adolf Hitler Brücke* had been blown, General Rose's patrols began to push quickly into the heart of the ruined city, dominated by those twin spires of the stately cathedral.

That same morning General Koechling was relieved of his command and arrested, probably at the instigation of the Gauleiter. He was to stand trial, he was informed, not only for dereliction of duty but also for possible treason. Bitter but resigned, knowing that he had fought his best for Germany in two wars, Koechling asked permission to write his report before he was taken away. It was granted. Sick at heart, the Corps Commander predicted that it would be "only a question of hours" before the city and the great Hohenzollern Bridge across the Rhine would be captured. "Willingness to fight," he maintained, "has given way to resignation and apathy on the part of the command as well as the completely worn-out troops."[5] An hour later he placed himself in the custody of his chief-of-staff and was taken back across the Rhine to face an uncertain future.

The drive into the heart of Cologne continued...

There was a new obstacle now. Apart from sniper fire and the German shells coming in from over the Rhine to burst right in the heart of the city, killing both American and German alike, there were still some forty thousand citizens of Cologne (out of a pre-war population of half a million) camping in the cellars and basements of the shattered city. Now they burst from their holes and hiding places to welcome the Americans as if they were liberators and not conquerors. "We've been waiting for you to come for a long time!"[6] one shabby man called out to US war correspondent Iris Carpenter. Many of them attempted to shake hands with the other correspondents who flooded in after the 3rd. Some pointed derisively to a big stencilled sign that the Civil Affairs crew had already put up in both English and German in front of the bomb-shattered opera house. It read:

GIVE ME FIVE YEARS AND YOU WILL
NOT RECOGNIZE GERMANY AGAIN.
Adolf Hitler

How very true; and many correspondents made a point of photographing civilians gesturing at the big black and white sign. But at
that moment the tankers were less concerned with propaganda than
with fighting their way through rubble, snipers and civilians towards
the vital bridge. There was a last dramatic tank battle right below the
shadow of the *Dom* itself, with two Shermans being knocked out
before their opponent, a German Mark IV, shared the same fate in the
debris surrounding the cathedral.

But they were not destined to take their bridge either. Hodges' First
Army was also to suffer failure. Just as they reached the approaches to
the bridge, pushing through that nightmarish lunar landscape behind
the main station, they came to a halt.

In front of them stretched the slow broad brown snake of the
Rhine. But their prize was gone. A huge 1,200 foot gap had been
blown in the Hohenzollern bridge and now its central spans lay in the
water. There was no point wasting any more lives. The race had come
to an abrupt end and already German guns on the far bank were rang-
ing in on the Americans. They withdrew.

In Hodges' sector of the Rhine front there was now only one bridge
left standing, and no one thought it might be of any use; after all, it
was a railway bridge.

On the afternoon of the next day Australian war correspondent Alan
Moorehead, a veteran of half a dozen campaigns since the war had
started, motored up with his wife to visit the newly captured city.

He didn't much like what he saw. There was no sound except the
occasional mortar shell whining over the debris on the opposite bank
of the Rhine. Every now and again a German civilian scurried out of a
broken doorway into another broken doorway. A group of soldiers
backed a truck up to a cellar and began carrying out cases of wine.
Someone was saying, "There are forty thousand Germans living
underground here and they have hoards of food and clean tablecloths
and flowers on the table."[7]

Miserable for some reason he couldn't quite explain, Moorehead
and his wife sat down in the spring sunshine on the banks of the Rhine
and ate chicken sandwiches on the Cathedral steps.

"All that was left of the building opposite was the sign '4711' – the name of the finest Eau de Cologne. Two drunks lurched by. All around us, acre after acre, the rubble lay in the sunshine, so real and solid that it seemed that Cologne had always been like that, and that there was no sense of pattern any more in anything. We were glad to leave."[8]

But back in the press camp, Moorehead's mood changed. "While we had been in Cologne, something had been happening farther upstream which had been enough to revive anyone's faith in life, even in war. A Lieutenant Timmermann, finding himself at the approaches to an unsmashed bridge at Remagen, had simply taken a deep breath and led his men across. This was the last bridge across the Rhine, the only one which the Germans had not exploded. No one had dreamed that we could "bounce" a bridge. But here he was on the opposite bank, Lieutenant Timmermann with half his army pouring across behind him. What a wonderful play it will make some day!"[9]

The slow, ponderous plodder General Hodges had done it at last. After six long months, the River Rhine had finally been crossed!

PART II

The most famous bridge in the world

We're gonna have a party on the Rhine!
Dwight D. Eisenhower, March 1945

ONE

It was the usual busy evening at the Goldenrod Café in West Point, Nebraska. The place was full of high school kids, drinking their evening milk shakes and listening to swing music blaring from the vibrating, multicoloured juke-box. It was a typical evening in the tail-end of the war in a typical American small town. The only signs that there was a war on were the recruiting posters pinned to one wall and the fact that the café's customers had all arrived on foot, for gasoline was rationed and the automobiles stayed at home.

Standing behind the counter, Bill Schaefer, who once had been known as Wilhelm Schäfer, the bald-headed owner of the café, grunted angrily when the phone started to jingle. He hated that phone. It always seemed to ring when he was at his busiest, and invariably one of his short-order cooks or waitresses had to drop whatever they were doing to answer it. Worst of all were the long-distance calls from Omaha, in wartime they took a devil of a time to get through, so he had to make his customers be quiet till the two parties concerned could speak. An this one turned out to be exactly that.

"Long distance for Mrs Mary Timmermann, Omaha calling!" the operator sang out, as the disgruntled proprietor took the phone off the hook.

Schaefer turned to a well-built, middle-aged waitress serving at one of the booths. "Timmy!" he called above the racket from the juke-box. "Get this phone again. Make it snappy! You got lots of customers."

Mrs Timmermann, known as "Timmy", bustled anxiously across the room. She was a little wary of phones. Her English wasn't so good and she was always afraid the telephone might bring her bad news. After all, she had two sons fighting in Germany and a daughter in the WACs.

Hesitantly she picked up the receiver and started to jabber away in her fractured, heavily accented English until a stern voice snapped, "Are you Mrs Mary Timmermann, the mother of Second-Lieutenant Karl H. Timmermann?"

Mrs Timmermann's heart missed a beat. Was this it? Had Karl been killed in action? He had already been wounded once, in the Ardennes only three months before. Had the worst happened now? White and shaking, she handed the phone over to her impatient boss and said, "Bill, help me, it's something about Karl. I don't know what."

Schaefer shook his bald head unsympathetically and took the phone. "Hello," he said. "What is it?"

"This is the Omaha *World-Herald* calling," an authorative voice answered. "Would you tell Mrs Timmermann that her son Second-Lieutenant Karl H. Timmermann has just crossed the Remagen Bridge – and he was the first officer over the bridge."

Schaefer knew where the Remagen bridge was all right; after all, he had been born on the Rhine himself. But still he couldn't figure why the newspaper man was making such a fuss about it. He thrust the phone back at an anxious Mrs Timmermann. "Here, take the phone, Timmy," he said impatiently. "Karl is all right. He just crossed the Remagen Bridge, that's all. Now talk to the man."

The newspaperman repeated the information and when the frightened, middle-aged waitress didn't respond, he asked, 'Do you know what it means?"

"I know what it means to me," Mrs Timmermann replied. "Is he hurt?"

"No, he's not hurt," the man in Omaha replied. "But listen to this. Karl Timmermann was the first officer of an invading army to cross the Rhine River since Napoleon."[1]

"Napoleon I don't care about," Mrs Timmermann retorted. "How is my Karl?"[2]

"It was the most romantic story of the campaign," Moorehead had exclaimed[3] when he heard the great news that same afternoon in far-off Cologne. But the Australian journalist did not then know the full extent of this "romantic story". Not only had a handful of brave men captured the first bridge across the Rhine at Remagen and held it, but their Army Commander General Bradley had made a snap decision, that same cold wet March day, to take the wind out of Montgomery's sails. He would upstage his rival's great set-piece Rhine crossing, still nearly three weeks off, by throwing over division after division to make the Remagen crossing not only a mere bridgehead on the eastern bank of the river, but a major thrust!

But the supreme irony of the whole story was that the young man who unwittingly changed the whole strategy of the last six weeks of World War Two in North-Western Europe had first seen the light of day not more than a hundred kilometres from that railway bridge, "the most famous bridge in the world", as the newspapers back home in the States were soon calling it. Karl H. Timmermann had been born in Germany!

Back in December 1918, Pfc Deane J. McAlister of the 2nd US Infantry Division had been the first American soldier to cross the River Rhine at Remagen as a member of the US Army of Occupation. He had been marching from France and through the Rhineland for nearly a fortnight, weighed down with eighty pounds of equipment, and as he recalled many years later, "My powers of observation were somewhat dimmed after twelve days of continuous hiking. I did not even see the bridge as we approached and the first thing I knew someone said, "We're on the Rhine!" and the platoon commander ordered us to break step. Then there was a mix-up at the head of the column and we halted in the middle of the bridge. They had the railroad tracks planked over so we could march over more easily."[4]

As 1918 gave way to 1919, the father of the man who would have to fight his way across that same railway bridge at Remagen, John H. Timmermann, a private in the 8th Infantry Regiment, crossed and became a member of the US Occupation Force. Unlike McAlister, John Timmermann, who was of German parentage and spoke good German, decided he'd stay a while longer in the Fatherland. He deserted from the US garrison outside Koblenz on the Rhine and crossed over into unoccupied Germany where the US military police had no authority. In due course he found a "war bride" in the city of Frankfurt and remained there as a deserter wanted by the US Army.

But Germany in the lean post-war years was no place for an American deserter. Unable to find work, virtually starving, the Timmermann family – now including young Karl, born in Frankfurt – decided they would go to the States, even if it meant imprisonment for

John. There were plenty of complications, but British and American Quakers took up the Timmermann case and finally after five years, in 1924, when Karl was a strapping three-year-old infant, they were allowed to return to the States. There, in the shadow of his disgraced father, who was given to boasting how he had "outsmarted" the US Army – meaning that he had escaped imprisonment for desertion – Karl grew up on the wrong side of the tracks in West Point, Nebraska, his father's home state. His father never settled down to a regular job and his mother had to go to work in a café, taking in laundry at night, in order to feed her family of three children.

Funnily enough, although local gossip had it that John Timmermann was a "yellow-bellied coward who deserted under fire on the front line",[5] Karl was attracted to the US Army. Even as an average high school student he studied weapons and tactics, and as soon as he was of age he left home – on June 24th, 1940, his eighteenth birthday – and joined up for three years. Later he would claim cynically that he had only joined "because all the garbage can lids froze down" and he wanted to eat.

Three years later Karl was commissioned into the infantry, posted to the 9th Armored Division, and sent overseas with that formation in August 1944. In his first action during the Battle of the Bulge in December 1944, when his green division was badly mauled just outside the Belgian town of St Vith, he was wounded.

So in this first week of March 1945, as his Division fought towards the Rhine, the newly appointed company commander Karl Timmermann had no illusions about war and combat. As he wrote home to his young wife in the States about that time, "There's no glory in war. Maybe those who have never been in battle find that there is a certain glory and glamour that doesn't exist. Perhaps they get it from the movies or the comic strips."[6]

And yet, for a few brief instants, Karl Timmermann – German born, with uncles fighting against him in the Wehrmacht – was going to achieve more glamour and glory than he ever could have imagined even in his wildest dreams. He was going to be the first American officer to cross the Rhine in combat – *and stay there*.

Of all the Rhine bridges still standing, the Ludendorff Railway Bridge at Remagen had never even been considered as a crossing point. The roads on the western bank leading into the Rhenish town were poor and on the other side any attacker would be faced with

600-foot sheer cliffs rising straight up from the Rhine. Beyond there were the forests of the Westerwald, traversed by dirt roads, fairly useless for an armoured drive. All the same, *any* bridge across the Rhine would greatly prized, for the prestige and publicity it would bring the Commanding General whose troops managed to seize it.

On March 4th, General Hodges began to discuss the possibility of capturing the Remagen bridge with General Millikin, commander of the US III Corps, to which the 9th Armored Division belonged. Both agreed it seemed pretty remote, now that the Germans had been alerted by the Ninth Army's attempts to seize the bridges of Uerdingen and Oberkassel.

Two days later, however, on the 6th, the Remagen bridge was still standing; and with the men of the 9th Armored just beyond the line of hills fringing the river's western bank at Remagen, there was renewed talk of dropping paratroopers on the other side or attempting to capture it by using a special force of Rangers, the American commandos. But as yet no one had given a clear order to capture the Remagen bridge.

In fact there was one general who was worried about the Remagen bridge: General von Zangen, commander of the German Fifteenth Army. His army was successfully defending a long section of the Siegfried Line twenty-five miles west of Remagen. He had no fears about his men losing ground to the Americans at present pushing up through the Eifel-Moselle area. But he did worry about his neighbour, the Fifth Panzer Army.

He had recurrent nightmares about General Hodges' First US Army bursting through the Fifth, which had been pressed right up against the Rhine, and seizing the Remagen bridge from the rear. He asked his chief, monocled Field-Marshal Model, who would shoot himself before the spring was out, to withdraw three of his divisions from the Siegfried Line to plug the breach.

Model did not approve. The man who had once been known as "the Führer's fire-brigade", because of his ability to dampen explosive battle situations, barked sarcastically: "How can you justify such a drastic relocation of forces, *Herr General?*"

"The Americans would have to be stupid not to take advantage of this hole and push tanks towards the Rhine. I think they will use this valley – like water flowing downhill."

"That's nonsense!" Model snapped, his notorious bad temper flaring up immediately. Only a fool would try to cross the Rhine where the cliffs rose steeply on the opposite bank. "None of your troops will be withdrawn from the *Westwall!*".[7,8]

So the bridge was left virtually undefended, save for a handful of engineers, members of the local home guard and a few infantrymen. It was a fatal oversight. For against all military good sense, the Americans would indeed attempt to cross there at the bridge at Remagen.

Late on the morning of March 7th, 1945, Lieutenant Timmermann's A Company of the 9th Armored Division's Combat Command B found itself in an abandoned German Labour Corps camp on the winding, narrow Birresdorf road situated on the heights just above Remagen. Two miles away the Remagen bridge was still intact, with men and vehicles from von Zangen's Army crossing it in a steady stream. For a while A Company was stalled because the road led on through some suspiciously silent woods, the ideal place for an ambush. But after Staff Sergeant Joseph de Lisio, a dynamic little New Yorker from the Bronx, appeared on the scene, the column started to move again. And then there it was.

As the column turned a sharp bend in the hills, down far below spread out as far as the eye could see, there was the silver snake of the great river and the town of Remagen. One of the men, Acting Sergeant Carmine Sabia, another New Yorker, cried in awe, "Jesus, look at that!" Then he asked another soldier: "*Do you know what the hell river that is?*"[9]

Back at the command post of General Hodges' Combat Command B, in the little town of Meckeneheim, the tall, strict commander was just studying his map with a magnifying glass when his divisional commander, General Leonard, walked in.

"How's it going?"Leonard asked in his usual informal manner.

Hodges, who had been at Omaha Beach and had fought all through the Battle of the Bulge, pointed to the map covered with its usual rash of blue and red crayon marks. "How about this bridge across the river?" he said, drawing a circle around the Remagen bridge.

"What about it?"

"Your intelligence can't tell me if it's still standing. Suppose I find that the bridge hasn't been blown here, should I take it?"

"Hell, yes," Leonard answered easily. "Go across it."

Just at that moment the commanding general noticed one of his staff officers beginning to buckle on his pistol. "Where the hell are you going?" he demanded.

"If Engeman is supposed to cross that bridge, somebody better tell him," the staff officer answered, referring to the colonel commanding the task force to which Timmermann's company belonged. "I don't think we ought to put it on the horn. It's too close to the Krauts."

Leonard grinned. "Yeah," he quipped, "go up there and maybe you'll get your name in the papers."

"General, I don't want my name in the papers," the staff officer replied, grabbing his helmet. "I just want to finish the damn war and go home!"[10]

It was a sentiment shared by Timmermann and his men as they edged their way into Remagen, fingers tense on the triggers of their weapons, heads swivelling constantly as they watched for snippers. The glory and prestige they could leave to the generals; they were only concerned with keeping alive. There was little danger for them on this side of the river; most of the enemy had already withdrawn, abandoning their makeshift street barricades. Still, they were taking no chances as they approached the bridge. They kept well tucked in behind the company of tanks to their front, The tanks had a nice thick steel hide; they just had soft, all-too soft, human flesh to protect them. But their slow careful progress was going to end soon.

General Hodges had arrived on the scene. Catching up with Colonel Engeman on the heights above Remagen, he was angered to find his task force stalled and Remagen apparently uncaptured. He asked Engeman impatiently why he hadn't already taken the little Rhenish town. Engeman tried to explain, but the tall, craggy-faced General had no time this day for explanations. Harshly he ordered the Colonel to get moving again – with all speed. Suddenly he remembered what Leonard had said to him earlier. Almost as if to himself, he muttered, "Be nice to have that bridge . . ."[11]

This was the opportunity Colonel Engeman had been waiting for. "*Yessir!*" he snapped hastily and hurried away to relay the order to Timmermann by radio.

The race to capture what would soon become "the most famous bridge in the world" was on.

2

By two o'clock that afternoon, Timmermann's company had cleared out most of the opposition in Remagen and were turning their attention on the bridge itself, which lay at the opposite end of the town, beyond the railway station. Now Timmermann's superior officer, Major Deevers, appeared and together they crouched in the smoking rubble, out of the way of the constant cross-fire, surveying the situation.

"Do you think you can get your company across that bridge?" Deevers asked at last, lowering his glasses.

"Well, we can try, sir," Timmermann answered, noting that most of the firing was coming from the red-brick bridge towers at the other side of the Rhine.

"Go ahead!" the Major snapped.

At that very moment a salvo of shells exploded on the bridge's superstructure. To Timmermann it appeared that the whole bridge would collapse under their impact. "What if it blows up in my face?" he asked anxiously.

Deevers had no answer for him.

Timmermann doubled across to his waiting men and rapped out his orders to his noncoms. None of them liked the idea of crossing the bridge, but Timmermann was not brooking any hesitation. "Orders are orders," he snapped. "We're told to go. All right, *Let's go!*"[12]

But there was no dramatic rush to capture the Remagen bridge. Unlike the handsome, virile heroes in the film version of the episode a quarter of a century later, the bearded, dirty GIs of Timmermann's company thought the assignment looked like sudden death – and were hesitant. Their stomachs were queasy, too; for some of them had been drinking wine looted from the inns along the riverside. But gradually, strung out into platoons, they started to creep through the drifting smoke down the slight slope leading to the twin towers on the western side.[13]

Major Deevers watched them move off. "Come on, fellers!" he called after them. "I'll see you on the other side and we'll all have a chicken dinner!"

As was to be expected, his remark drew many an obscene retort from the infantrymen about what the good Major could do with his chicken dinner.

Deevers flushed angrily. "*Move on!*" he yelled fiercely. "Get going!"[14]

They were almost at the bridge now. The battalion chaplain, with typical American interest in obtaining a good souvenir, prepared to film the crossing with an 8 mm camera. Bullets began to howl off the steel girders and chip at the brickwork ...

Timmermann, face flushed and angry, kept urging his men to greater efforts. In the lead, Staff Sergeant de Lisio rushed the right tower. He discovered five frightened Germans huddled around a jammed Spandau machine gun. He blasted off two shots against the wall with his MI. *"Hände hoch!"* he yelled – unnecessarily, as it turned out, for the surprised Germans were already throwing their hands into the air, faces ashen with fright.

Pushing the Germans ahead of him, the stocky little non-com clambered up the stairs to the tower's second chamber. Two men stood there, one of them as officer, apparently drunk. He tried to stagger to the detonating device in the corner. De Lisio ripped off a burst in front of his feet, then pushed him and the other German down the stairs.

Meanwhile tall lanky Alex Drabik was looking for de Lisio. Knowing just how aggressive the Italo-American was, Drabik reasoned the Sergeant had run into the railway tunnel ahead. "De Lisio must be over there, all alone!" he yelled to his companions. "Let's go!"

Running so fast that his helmet fell off – General Hodges himself later found it on the bridge – Drabik raced for the tunnel. He was followed by an excited, frightened, one-time plasterer from Minnesota, Marvin Jensen, who kept shouting, *"Holy crap, do you think we'll make it? ... Do you think we'll make it?"*[15]

Drabik wasn't listening, however. He was too concerned about reaching the tunnel. And then he was there. Alex Drabik, with his long haggard Slavic face, had made it. He had become the first American to cross the Rhine on active duty in World War Two – *and stay there.*

A few moments later a gasping Lieutenant Karl Timmermann, the German-born American, had joined him, the first American officer to have crossed the Rhine. At last he had removed the blemish on the family name incurred when his father had crossed the Rhine himself so long before and "gone over the hill". In a curious, ironic way, Karl Timmermann had returned home.[16]

TWO

At last, six months after Montgomery had first attempted to "bounce the Rhine" in the ill-fated Arnhem operation, the Allies had finally crossed Germany's greatest remaining natural barrier.

"It was a moment for history!" *Time* magazine proclaimed jubiliantly that week in March. "It is the biggest military triumph since Normandy!" the Associated Press correspondent cabled home.

But in the midst of all the celebrations and self-congratulation, one thing seemed to have been forgotten. It was not Field-Marshal Montgomery and his Britons who had captured the Remagen bridge; it was the American generals, who hated and envied him, who had succeeded where he had failed.

As yet, however, no top-level decisions had been made which would turn that bold capture of the Remagen bridge into something more than a desperate *coup de main* carried out by a group of obscure infantrymen.

On the German side, confused though the situation was, the reaction was quick. Hitler's Chief-of-Staff, Colonel General Alfred Jodl, heard the dread news on the day of his second marriage to a secretary half his age. They had just eaten the wedding supper of cold cuts, lettuce and pudding, their table decorated with flowers sent personally by the Führer, when the phone rang.

It was General Westphal, Chief-of-Staff West. While Jodl listened intently to what the sharp young staff officer had to say, his new bride noticed her husband's normally pale face turn red. Jodl ran his hand through his thinning hair and exclaimed, "At Remagen? ... *But it's not possible!*" He paused for a moment and listened, then said, "Yes, yes, I'll tell the Führer. Goodbye." He put the phone down and put both hands on his new bride's shoulders. "Patton has crossed the Rhine at Remagen with his tanks. And that on our wedding day! Now I must go. It will be late before I get back, but I'll bring you a couple of rolls from the vegetarian kitchen."[1] With that he was gone, leaving Luise Jodl to clear away the table. Sadly she told herself that he and she had crossed a bridge, too – a bridge into the unknown.

There was no hope for her or Germany now. Within two months her new husband would be a prisoner-of-war, accused of being a war criminal. Within a year or so, he would be dead, hanged by the neck at Nuremberg.

In spite of the Remagen crossing, the German High Command ordered that all positions *west* of the Rhine should be held and the first scattered improvised units were rushed to contain the new bridgehead. Meanwhile, back at Spa in Belgium, Hodges was hesitating. Should he break with agreed strategy and reinforce his bridgehead at Remagen? The terrain and the road network were terrible. Besides, there was Montgomery's great set-piece crossing in the north to be considered. In the end Hodges compromised. He ordered his staff to ready all available units to move up to the bridge and then called his superior, General Bradley, with the startling news.

"*A bridge?* You mean you've got one intact on the Rhine?" Bradley asked from his château headquarters at Namur, Belgium. "Really?"

Hodges assured him that he had.

"Hot dog, Courtney, this will bust him wide open!" Bradley cried. "Are you getting the stuff across?"

"I'm going to give it everything I've got," Hodges told him, realizing that he already had Bradley's approval.

"Shove everything you can across it, Courtney, and button the bridgehead up tightly,"[2] Bradley ordered, knowing now that this would be the way to stop Eisenhower taking away from Hodges' First Army ten divisions needed to fight on other fronts, not commanded by himself.

So Bradley himself was now committed. He had ordered Hodges to push division after division across the Rhine at Remagen. But he had not yet obtained Eisenhower's permission for a move that would effectively change the whole strategy of the war in the west. Even as night fell and he went to dinner, he had still not telephoned Eisenhower to tell him what he had done.

Bradley's sole guest that night was Eisenhower's operations officer,

General Harold "Pink" Bull. Bull was surprised. He had heard the news of the successful crossing as soon as he reached Bradley's HQ. Yet the Army Group commander did not mention the subject once throughout the meal, although Bull himself could think of little else but the bridge at Remagen. And, not knowing that Bradley had not yet informed his boss what he had done, Bull wondered what Eisenhower thought of the whole business.

After the meal the two old friends went into the war room, where Bull told Bradley bluntly: "You're not going anywhere down there at Remagen ... Besides, it just doesn't fit into the overall plan."

Bradley exploded at that. "Plan, hell! A bridge is a bridge and mighty damn good *anywhere* across the Rhine!'

Bull attempted to calm him. "I was only saying that Remagen wasn't the ideal position to cross that we've been looking for."

Suddenly Bradley calmed down a little. "I don't want you to give up your plan," he exclaimed. "Just let us develop this crossing with four or five divisions. Perhaps you can use it as a diversion? Or maybe we can employ it to strengthen our pincers south of the Ruhr. At any rate it's a crossing. We've gotten over the Rhine. But now that we've got a bridgehead, for God's sake let's use it."

"But once you get across, Brad," Bull persisted, "where do you go?"

Bradley explained his troops could thrust north towards the autobahn, then swing south-east to Frankfurt; in other words, breaking completely with the original plan which would have had Allied troops forming a pincer movement around the Ruhr.

Bull didn't like it; he said it would be difficult to change the overall plan, drawn up nearly a year before. Then suddenly it dawned on him. *Bradley had not told Eisenhower yet about the bridge at Remagen, although the news was already two hours old!* He stared hard at Bradley and said firmly, "You can talk to me all night, Brad, and it won't make any difference. I can't give you permission to send four or five divisions across."[3]

Now it was up to Bradley to inform Eisenhower.

Far away at his palatial residence in Rheims, France, once the home of one of the local "champagne barons", Eisenhower was dining with the airborne generals who were his guests that night. He had just complained that the soup didn't taste too good when he was summoned to the phone in the next room. General Bradley wished to speak to him urgently. He excused himself and the guests grew silent, no doubt wondering what was so important that the Supreme Commander should be interrupted in this manner. After all, senior officers were never disturbed at "chow" in the US Army.

Commander Harry Butcher, Eisenhower's personal assistant, was one of those at the dinner party that Wednesday night. Although "Ike" was in the next room, he later recorded, he could hear every word his chief was saying. "Brad, that's wonderful!" he exclaimed. There was a pause, then he continued: "Sure, get right on across with everything you've got. It's the best break we've had ... To hell with the planners! Sure, go on Brad, and I'll give you everything we got to get to hold that bridgehead. We'll make good use of it even if the terrain isn't too good."

A few moments later Eisenhower reappeared and gave the assembled brass one of his famous ear-to-ear grins. "Hedges got a bridge at Remagen and already has troops across!"

As Butcher later commented: "Bradley had wanted to be sure it was OK to exploit and as usual they were in quick and complete agreement."[4]

Another guest at that dinner, General "Slim Jim" Gavin – commander of the 82nd Airborne Division and one of the few generals present who was not anti-Montgomery – saw it differently. "The seizure of the crossing at Remagen," he wrote, thirty years after Harry Butcher's account, "suggested to General Bradley ... a 'Bradley Plan' that envisioned a direct thrust to the east to link up with the Soviets.

"This would obviate the need to give American divisions to Montgomery and would relegate Montgomery and his Army Group to a secondary role.

"The capture of the Remagen bridge and Eisenhower's prompt decision to exploit the crossing was a historic event of extraordinary importance. It would allow General Eisenhower to give free rein to his own generals: Bradley, Patton, Hodges and Simpson ... But for it to be carried out successfully, *it was important that the details of the plan should not be disclosed to the British until it was an accomplished fact*" (author's italics).[5]

But Eisenhower changed his mind. One day later, he ordered Bradley to tell Hodges he could only expand the Remagen bridgehead 1,000 yards a day and when finally he did reach the Bonn-Frankfurt autobahn, he was to wait there until he received the green light from SHAEF.

On March 13th, Eisenhower went even further. He radioed Bradley that Hodges should not be allowed to advance more than ten miles. The Remagen bridgehead should be used solely to draw German troops away from the Ruhr and those facing Montgomery, now preparing for his great crossing of the Rhine.

But by now the American generals were already committed to what Gavin called the "Bradley Plan". And Bradley, whom Churchill once described as "a sour-faced bugger who would not listen",[6] was determined not to be left out of this last great battle of the Rhine. What was more, he had one man under his command who he was sure would back him up right to the hilt, whether "Ike" liked it or not – General George Patton Jr.

"My favorite general is George S. Patton," the American publicist Dwight MacDonald wrote back in 1944. "Some of our generals like Stilwell have developed a sly ability to simulate human beings. But Patton always behaves as a general should. His side arms (a brace of pearl-handled revolvers) are as clean as his tongue is foul. He wears special uniforms which, like Goering, he designs himself and which are calculated like the ox-horns worn by ancient Gothic chieftains to strike terror into the enemy (and any rational person for that matter)."[7]

Pretty powerful stuff for a war-winning General, leading the biggest field army the United States had ever sent overseas. But to a superficial observer Patton did indeed epitomize the tough, rough, brawling masculine figure that one associates with American frontier tradition. With a nickname like "Old Blood an' Guts" how should he be otherwise? He was indeed violent and vulgar, concerned with getting the right sneer on his thin lips as he pulled what he called his "war face number one". He liked to impart the image of the pistol-packin' general, whose language was well salted with "goddam", "sonuvabitches" and much worse.

One new division going into the line was told by their Army Commander, "The way most new soldiers use their rifles, they are no more use than a pecker is to the Pope!" Another division was told, "All this bull about thinking of your mother and your sweetheart and your wives is emphasized by [what] writers who have never heard a hostile shot or missed a meal think battle is. Battle is the most magnificent competition in which a human being can indulge. It brings out all that is best; it removes all that is base ... Americans pride themselves on being he-men and they *are* he-men!"[8]

But there was more to General George Patton than loud-mouthed braggadocio. Arrogant, aristocratic, utterly un-American in his attitude to those values which his fellow countrymen regarded as democratic and typically American, he had not come from the lower middle classes like most of his fellow generals. He had been born into a family that was independently wealthy. As a newly married young lieutenant, he and his wife were accustomed to dress for dinner and thus earned themselves the malicious, perhaps envious, nickname of "the Duke and Duchess".

After distinguished service in the First War, he could afford to run the latest, most luxurious automobiles – and this was at a time when only one sedan was allowed officially in the whole of the US Army: that of the Commander-in-Chief. In the depressed 1930s, when Eisenhower and Bradley and the rest were glad if they had enough money to afford an old Model T, Patton was in a position to run a whole stable of polo ponies, billeting them at the nearest livery stable at more cost per horse than the average American was earning at that time.

In short, Patton's way of life prior to World War Two had more in common with an independently wealthy British cavalry officer in one of the "better" regiments than with any of his fellow American officers. His style, too, was definitely un-American. There was no informality about General Patton. One had to be at least an army commander before one dared to call him "George" or "Georgie". The American novelist John Marquand observing him at dinner at his grand HQ in Sicily in 1943, noted: "It was a very good dinner too, faintly reminiscent of grownups and children's tables at a Thanksgiving party. The Generals were grownups, the staff officers the children."[9]

And those "children", the staff officers, fawned upon him like eager sycophantics. Colonel Codman, for example, a well-travelled, educated man of some wealth who was one of his aides, wrote of him at the time: "He [Patton] has contributed to the science of warfare professional proficiency of the highest modern order. More significantly, however, and this is that which sets him apart, he brings to the art of command in this day and age the norms and antique virtues of the classic warrior ... In the time of Roger the Norman or in ancient Rome, General Patton would have felt completely at home."[10] Fulsome praise indeed – and Codman was not alone. Patton's one-eyed Chief-of-Staff "Hap" Gay called him "the bravest man I know".

Patton thoroughly enjoyed being surrounded by admirers and devotees of his style of command. Correspondents loved him. He was always good for a ribald story and an apt, bold quote. Reading through the yellowing newspapers of that time, there seems hardly an issue without General Patton's name on the front page. As Commander Butcher, who was in charge of Eisenhower's own publicity, recorded at the time: "If the correspondents with the Third Army [Patton's command] don't mention Patton, apparently the headline writers back home insert his name. In any event, Patton is getting greater publicity and is overshadowing Hodges of the US First Army. I have 'made a signal' to the PRO of First Army suggesting that the correspondents there be encouraged to write of that army as Hodges. This may balance the credit. But it takes a lot of color in any man to balance Patton."[11]

This March, however, not only had Hodges hogged the headlines through his crossing of the Rhine at Remagen, but soon Patton's hated rival Montgomery was going to do the same. And Patton didn't like it. In his over-fertile imagination it seemed to him that everyone was against him, trying to prevent him obtaining the glory he thought was his due. Had he not in previous ages (Patton believed in reincarnation) been a Roman centurion, a Viking warrior, etcetera, etcetera, always fighting for the honour and the glory of the particular civilization and country to which he had belonged at the time? But fighting not only against the enemy outside, but the enemy *within* – those who wished to prevent him doing his duty. As he had once quipped back in London the previous year, when he was in disgrace for having slapped two reluctant American soldiers who had refused to fight in Sicily, and he was having to attend hospital for treatment for a growth on his mouth: "After all the ass-kissing I have to do, no wonder I have a sore lip!"

Now, given Bradley's approval, Patton was determined that he too would cross the Rhine. There was only one problem. On the very same day that Karl Timmermann crossed the bridge at Remagen, Patton's Third Army was still bogged down in the fighting in the Eifel-Moselle area, some sixty miles away from the Rhine. If he and Bradley were going to beat Montgomery and "take the Rhine on the run" as the Field-Marshal urged, he would have to force crossings of both the rivers Moselle and Saar; fight his way through the *Vulkaneifel*, the "Volcanic Eifel", the rugged hilly area between Wittlich and Gerelstein formed from extinct volcanoes; and then, if he had sufficient bridging equipment (for there were no bridges left standing along the Rhine in Third Army's area of operations), make an assault crossing of the great river itself. It was going to be a tall order, even for General "Blood an' Guts" Patton.

THREE

Once in a moment of drunken exuberance, Patton had declared to his nephew Fred Ayres: "The soldier who won't fuck won't fight!"[1]

Now the men of his Third Army beginning to battle their way through the Eifel hills and down the Moselle valley towards the Rhine did both – they fucked and they fought. Just like the French, the English, the Spaniards and the Swedes who had preceded them over the centuries, forcing the forefathers of many of these same GIs to flee for the better life of the New World, they brought with them terror and sudden death.

The speed of Patton's advance caught the Germans by surprise. The local authorities had been unable to evacuate the civilians from the "red zone", as it was called, and carry out Hitler's vaunted scorched earth policy. Now everywhere Patton's soldiers were entering large inhabited German communities, all of them decked out with white flags, sheets, towels, grandpa's underpants – anything that indicated surrender – where they were welcomed by old men, women and children, mostly grateful that the war was over for them. They also found *girls!*

On March 1st, 1945, their Supreme Commander, General Eisenhower, had issued a "non-fraternization" ban. In a printed folder handed out to every American soldier, he stated: "You are entering Germany, not as a liberator, but as a victor. Do not keep smiling. Never offer a cigarette ... nor offer your hand. The Germans will respect you as long as they see in you a successor to Hitler who never offered them *his* hand ... *The only way to get along with the Germans is to make them respect you, to make them feel the hand of the master.*"[2]

Patton's reaction, as he once told Montgomery, was that "as long as a soldier keeps his helmet on and his elbows on the ground, it ain't fraternization – it's fornication!"[3] Now, however, his soldiers were living cheek-by-jowl with women in the tight little half-timbered houses of the Eifel and Moselle; and discipline in his Third Army started to get out of hand. "Pig Alley" (Place Pigalle) in Paris with its readily available girls was a long way away and tomorrow they might well be killed. So the GIs took their pleasures, if necessary, by force. The grandsons and great-grandsons of those humble peasants who had fled the Eifel-Moselle area for the *Land der unbegreznten Moglichkeiten* ("the land of unlimited possibilities"), as they had called it, came back to terrorize.

Forty years later, the parish chronicles of those remote villages still tell the violent story of Patton's push for the Rhine: the short, sharp fire-fight; the "Ami" artillery bombardment; the flight of the German defenders; the rumble of Sherman tanks and first cautious infantrymen, tossing grenades into cellars, beating down doors with their butts, crying all the while in broken German, "*Raus, raus ... mak schnell!*

Thereafter came the looting, the drinking and, if the officers lost control – which they often did, now that the GIs were out of the foxholes and could lose themselves in a village or township – rape and murder. One girl, watching the entry of units of the US 6th Armored Division into her home village that March, saw drunken infantrymen place some German prisoners in the big wooden manure casks used for taking the stuff out to the fields, then amuse themselves by firing at the feet of the terrified POWs to make them dance. Later they "rode a little horse to death" and looted the houses. Towards evening they roasted the looted chickens and got down to serious drinking. Soon they began to look for women. "Hello frowlein ... hello frowlein!" they cried as they searched the crowded hall into which they had herded the village's total population. The frightened villagers hid all the presentable girls underneath a big table. "Fortunately," the girl recorded later, "the two *Amis* were too drunk to see the girls' shoes sticking out so they passed and we were saved – for this night at least."[4]

Not all the local women were so fortunate. Following in the wake of the 76th Infantry Division, a relatively new outfit in the Third Army, which had had its baptism of fire in late January at the assault crossing of the river Sauer, there were numerous reports of rape and destruction. In the township of Wittlich, some twelve miles or so from the Moselle, on March 10th, the wife of a local schoolteacher was raped by four soldiers in the presence of her children; she later had to be placed in a mental home because of her treatment that day. A little further on at the village of Bausendorf, after a sharp exchange of fire, men of the same division were only prevented from raping the women in the local inn by a sudden artillery bombardment which set the place on fire.

Finally reaching the Moselle at Piesport, men of the 76th took over the houses lining the river and proceeded to loot their wine cellars. One small-time vintner there had his waterside premises taken over by young GIs who spent their days drinking and sniping at anything that moved on the other side. Naturally the German soldiers were too wary to move except at night-time, but the civilians were not so cautious. Thus it was that one day the horrified owner of the house watched as the amateur snipers spotted an aged civilian, draped in a bed sheet to show he was harmless and dragging a wooden cart behind him, and brought him down – though only after several attempts to do so, for their aim was not so steady. The old man lay there for three days before someone spirited him away.

As General Betts, in charge of Eisenhower's legal affairs, was to write after the war: "From the breakthrough at the Ruhr river in February 1945 until the cessation of hostilities, the trend [of crimes against civilians] again shows a sudden rise, hardly proportionate to the number of troops engaged."[5] Indeed from February to May, as US statistics reveal, there were five hundred cases of *convicted* rape a month.

But by his ruthless energy and constant driving, Patton kept his men moving forward despite all the temptations of loot and women in the Eifel-Moselle area. In the second week of March, his favourite armoured division, the 4th – which had brought Patton his first victories in Brittany and relieved Bastogne the previous December – burst forth from the Eifel and, leaving the infantry far behind, charged into the unknown, heading for the Rhine. Crossing the River Kyll at a remote little water-mill hidden in a valley, the 4th's Shermans dodged and twisted down the secondary roads of the Eifel, avoiding battle wherever possible till they came to the Moselle at Karden, bursting right through the German defenders and covering thirty-five miles in a mere two days.

Correspondent James Wellard with the Third Army described that tremendous advance thus: "One night Patton had been fighting in the Siegfried Line; the next he was on the Rhine sixty-five miles to the east. His tanks had just gone. They roared along the mountain roads in one of those terrifying maneuvers when they just disappear over some hilltop and are not heard of again for forty-eight hours. They had gone into the mountains and crossed rivers without the benefit of infantry, supply columns or supporting artillery. Now the head of this armored column was nearly a hundred miles in advance of the main infantry units. It stuck out on a long slender neck. On the maps, it looked impossible ... It was not only possible. It was brilliantly right ... The blitz of the 4th Armored Division represented the greatest action of the war!"[6]

It took its toll, however. Bennett H. Fishler, serving with the 8th Tank Battalion, wrote home to his wife after it was all over: "My three letters a week scheme sure went kaput for a while, but that is not because I didn't want to write. We've been on the run some considerable bit, as you know from the papers, and it's been all I could do to eat, much less sit down to a letter ... No German village is complete without the full set of white flags ... If there are any German soldiers around who wish to contest our entrance, the reception is a little different at first, although later on it amounts to the same thing, except the white flags fly from the rubble. Personally, I don't have a great deal of stomach for this town fighting business, even if they are Kraut towns, because it means that there are plenty of non-soldiers involved, but what is necessary, I suppose, is necessary."[7]

But the casualties incurred were not only German; nor were they always battle casualties in this tremendous armoured dash for the Rhine. At Karden, as the Americans prepared to cross, pensioner Heinz Rath was lined up at the river's edge with the rest of the menfolk, including his cousin. For some reason his cousin went a little mad and started to rave at the heavily armed GIs and threaten them with his fist. Rath just managed to prevent his cousin being shot there on the spot, as the Shermans started to roll towards the River Moselle, and hurriedly they got out of the way of the thirty-ton, mud-splattered monsters. But one GI was not so fortunate. He was crushed to death by a Sherman in the same instant that the German defenders on the hills opposite opened fire. Risking his own life, for the Sherman crew seemingly did not know that they had just killed one of their own men, Rath rushed forward and dragged the dead GI to cover. His reward, as he recalled many years later, was a pat on the back from an American sergeant and a bar of chocolate!

But in spite of the tankers' exhaustion and their casualties, Patton continued to push and push, 'chewing out' any officer, whatever his rank, if he thought he was holding up the race for the Rhine. Once he even threatened a divisional general that he'd make him swim across a river if he didn't find the necessary bridging equipment and get over. And in the end they did. The 4th finally reached the Rhine near the town of Andernach and soon linked up with its running-mate, the relatively inexperienced IIth US Armored Division, which had had a hard job to keep up.

Now it was the turn of the infantry. It would be their job to attack across the Moselle and clear the way for the exhausted tankers to race for the crossing sites on the Rhine which Patton had planned for his Third between Mainz and Mannheim. Again this would drag the whole of Allied strategy, after the Rhine had been successfully crossed, way to the south-east and away from the northern drive for Berlin. But such things did not worry Patton. His main concern now was to beat Montgomery.

On March 16th, with seven days to go before Montgomery was scheduled to attack, Patton started stage two of his completely un-authorized campaign to cross the Rhine. Around the peacetime tourist town and beauty spot of Cochem, Patton's 5th and 89th In-fantry Divisions started attacking at dawn. At the same time, General Culin's 87th Infantry Division launched its attack on the great Rhen-ish city of Koblenz further upstream at the confluence of the Moselle and the Rhine.

At first the 87th Infantry Division met little resistance. Indeed, when a handful of SS men fired upon the Americans at the riverside village of Guels and were later taken prisoner, the Americans them-selves had to defend their prisoners against the enraged local popula-tion. The villagers, incensed that these young fools of the 6th SS Mountain Division still wanted to fight, had decided they would lynch the lot of them! But as the Americans pressed closer to the ruined city itself, the 1,800 defenders of *Kampfgruppe Koblenz*, aided by deadly air bursts from high velocity 88 mm flak guns stationed on the other side of the Rhine, put up a stout defence.

Pfc Lester Atwell, a medic who had served with Patton's Third

Army since Metz in November 1944, went over with the infantry but to his horror found himself trapped in a cellar with a handful of comrades from the medical team. Outside he and his friends could hear the Germans shouting as they searched the ruins for Americans. "My God," he thought, "how often could one go through this strain, this sensation of fear wrenching and bucketing up from the pit of one's stomach?" At any minute he expected the Germans to burst in, line them all up and shoot them. Up above one of the Germans spat. Footsteps crunched on the gravel. "Boots came down the backporch steps and rifle fire opened up in the yard beyond. The Germans at our cellar door moved up to join in."

After a long silence a voice whispered, "They're gone!" When nothing happened Atwell rose to his feet. A bone cracked. The others got to their feet, too, but they weren't leaving the protection of the cellar this night.

They had escaped with their lives once again, but as Atwell noted, the strain was telling on them and their infantry comrades, for in spite of the bursts of fire all around, "emotion had worn itself out."[8]

Throughout the next day the fighting in and around Koblenz continued. As fog settled over the shattered city the next night, the evacuation of most of the defenders was ordered. Silently they withdrew over the Rhine, leaving some five hundred SS men to defend a narrow strip of the bank. Of those five hundred, only fifty escaped, as the Americans pressed home their final attack on the 18th.

Atwell recorded the dying moments of the city. "The fall of a city the size and importance of Coblenz [sic]," he wrote in 1945, "was nothing as one had imagined it. The windows of all the houses were shuttered tight, a few dead Germans and American soldiers lay in the streets; jeeps raced by; artillery barrages screamed in, bringing houses down in a thunder of rubble; fighting continued from street to street. But there was, over all, the chaotic air of a drunken, end-of-the-world carnival. Infantrymen who had been down in the cellars ran crookedly past, firing anywhere and shrill, overexcited young German girls, impatient of rape, ran after them through barrages, ducking into almost flat doorways as tiles fell from the roofs in crashing showers.

"A Free French photographer drove up in a jeep, brandishing a revolver and staggered out drunk to take pictures. In a shattered house directly across the way from us we heard someone banging out 'Lili Marlene' on the piano, and going into a rage the photographer entered and pulled open the door with a shout. On the point of firing, he found himself staring at two American soldiers ... The photographer came over to us, shaking from his narrow escape ...

"In another house Jimmy McDonough and Horse-face Fogarty [two of Atwell's fellow aid-men] were looting the contents of a living-room. They had learned to say '*Achtung! Macht schnell! Kommen Sie hier!*' and approximations of several other German expressions that they repeated to each other over and over."

After a while Fogarty, with his back to McDonough and busy with his looting, got sick of the game. "Hey, cut it out, you make me nervous," he barked. "What the hell's the matter with you anyway, always fuckin' around ..." Then he felt something poke him in the back; and when he turned round he saw that Jimmy McDonough was at the far side of the room, speechless and shivering, his hands over his head. Four armed German soldiers had entered the room after them – but they had only come to surrender.

Further up the street, a war-weary Atwell entered another living-room. "A group of American soldiers were fast getting drunk. Going tipsily into the dark hall to look for the bathroom, they found themselves, in confusion, bumping into German soldiers who had been holding wassail on the second floor and had come downstairs on the same mission. 'Scuse me, Beg your pardon. Wanna get through here,' one American found himself saying to an equally drunken German in a polite, Alphonse-and-Gaston act."[9]

Outside as the 88 mm shells came screaming over and frightened German prisoners doubled by, hands on their heads, he saw one of his comrades copulating in the street with a German woman. Truly, he thought, this was the end of the world.

It was, for the German defenders. While Koblenz writhed in its death throes there were some 90,000 German soldiers on the loose, scattered and confused, in a triangle bounded by the rivers Rhine, Saar and Moselle. Their commander himself had narrowly missed being captured and had now taken up his "headquarters" in an old post office not far from Bad Kreuznach, his "signals organization" composed of a handful of brave women post office clerks who had remained behind at their posts when their male colleagues had fled and were whispering back reports of American troop movements.

The US Third Army had started on the last phase of its plan to cross the Rhine and beat Montgomery. Nothing, it seemed, could stop Patton now.

FOUR

On the same day that Koblenz fell, the man who was to command Montgomery's force crossing the Rhine met a select group of favourite correspondents some one hundred miles downstream. He was about to reveal his great plan.

Outside of the Army, the man who had led Montgomery's troops in battle right from the beginning back in June 1944, was little known. Montgomery had seen to that; he wanted all available publicity for himself. Besides, General Miles "Bimbo" Dempsey, commander of the British Second Army, had never courted publicity. Even his corps commanders, such as General Horrocks, were better known than he was.

Yet the forty-eight-year-old General with sloping shoulders and a small mobile mouth beneath his trim Army moustache, who rarely smiled, had had a remarkable career already, rising from a battalion commander in 1939 to army commander four short years later, having fought in the Desert, Syria, Sicily and Italy before landing in France. In the words of Captain Thompson, one of the favoured correspondents that day, Dempsey was "the unassuming commander of the most unassuming army in the world. Neither the commander nor the army seeks personal glory. They seek only to maintain their integrity and to win this war as swiftly as possible."[1]

The General strode back and forth in front of his caravan underneath the spring-budding trees – followed by his pet goose "Gertie of Falaise" – explaining his plans to the assembled correspondents and waving his hands in a somewhat un-English fashion to emphasize his words.

"We will cross the Rhine on the night of the 23rd," he stated. "Four corps are under my command. XXX Corps will cross in the north near Rees and continue northward for the capture of Emmerich. XII Corps will cross in the centre at Xanten, while the Commandos turn south to capture Wesel. On the following morning, the 18th United States Airborne Corps with the 6th British Airborne Division under command will drop near the Ijssel River on the opposite bank of the Rhine and secure the bridges there. Finally the VIII Corps will follow through and I cannot yet tell you how far they will go. The Ninth American Army will also attack on my right flank and proceed eastward along the Ruhr."[2]

None of the correspondents present that day noticed any hesitancy as the General he mentioned Simpson's Americans on his right flank. It had taken determined efforts, not only by General Simpson, but also by Dempsey himself, to have American troops involved in the great assault. Montgomery had wanted to make it an all-British attack, for obvious reasons, but still wished to retain Simpson's divisions for the follow-up. Finally, however, he had been persuaded – perhaps under the threat of having the whole of Simpson's Ninth Army taken away from him – to allow two American divisions, the 30th and 79th Infantry, to cross on Dempsey's flank.

After the fifteen-minute briefing there was a question-and-answer session. Veteran Australian war correspondent Alan Moorehead, who had seen war in ten different countries since 1939 and was heartily sick of it, asked only one: would this be the last battle, he wanted to know.

Dempsey, who hated rhetoric and melodrama, answered simply: "Yes."

Thereafter the correspondents adjourned for tea, a chance for an informal chat. At first they couldn't get near Dempsey, surrounded as he was by his staff officers, but presently he lowered his teacup and turned to the correspondents to ask, "Any of you know how 'Pop Goes the Weasel' goes?"

The correspondents considered, trying to reconstruct the old Cockney slang song about free-spending East Enders who had to pawn their belongings at the end of a jaunt – in other words, "popped the weasel". But why in heaven's name, they wondered, did the Army Commander want to know such a thing at this decisive moment.

In the end it was Thompson who, feeling slightly foolish, recited the words for Dempsey:

"Up and down the City Road,
In and out the Eagle.
That's the way the money goes,
Pop goes the Weasel!"

Dempsey thanked him gravely and turned back to his staff officers. "Suppose we sent: 'That's the way the money goes'," he said thoughtfully, "would Bert Harris get it?"

"In and out the Eagle might be better," one of them suggested.

But finally the signal sent to Bert Harris read simply: "That's the way the money goes." And "Bert" – otherwise Air Chief Marshal Sir Arthur Harris – understood all right. Soon his bomber command would fly their great attack on the Rhine and "pop" would go not the Weasel, but the great German city of Wesel . . .

Ever since December 1944, at the height of the Battle of the Bulge, Montgomery's planners had been working on preparations for the largest assault river crossing of all times: one that would rival the invasion of France itself in the number of troops involved, the supplies accumulated, the supporting firepower, and so on.

With 1,250,000 men under Montgomery's command from the Canadian, British and American armies, the Second British Army alone had accumulated 60,000 tons of ammunition, 30,000 tons of engineers' stores and 28,000 tons of other supplies. For its part, Simpson's Ninth Army had acquired 138,000 tons for the crossing. More than 37,000 British and Canadian engineers would be involved and 22,000 Americans. Over 5,500 guns of various calibres would fire the preliminary barrage. There would be 2,500 pontoons, 650 storm boats, 2,000 assault boats, 60 river tugs, 70 small tugs.

To the rear four new railheads had been built, scores of roads had been repaired and huge gangs of Dutch and Belgian labourers re-cruited to build new ones, while the local German inhabitants had been evacuated into Holland in case they betrayed the operation to German spies. And over all hung a chemical smoke-screen which would be kept up for ten long stinking days over a twenty-mile-long Rhine frontage, to conceal these massive preparations from the enemy waiting on the eastern bank of the Rhine. Every last detail had been arranged: from chemical heating pads borrowed from Army hospitals for wrapping round the outboard motors of the assault craft to ensure that they would start immediately in the damp spring weather of the Lower Rhine, to contraceptives - "rubbers" to the GIs, "French letters" to the Tommies – for covering the muzzles of their rifles so that they would not rust up and misfire on the day. Nothing had been forgotten. But in the final analysis, in the midst of this enormous technical and mechanical build-up, everything depended upon the soldier who was going to do the assaulting. On the day, it was the ordinary "Canuck", "Jock", "Tommy" or "Dough" who would decide whether Germany's last great natural bastion would be forced or not.

On a beautiful summer's evening, June 12th, 1940, the buglers of the 51st Highland Division – what was left of it – blew the "Cease-Fire" at the battered French port of St Valery. There was nothing left to fight with and nothing left to fight for. The British Navy could no longer evacuate the surviving Jocks of General Fortune's 51st Highland Division, "Scotland's pride". Thus some 8,000 men of the 51st, which had gained such a great reputation in the Great War, gave in to an obscure German general named Rommel and disappeared behind the wire for the rest of the war. The Division had been wiped out in two short weeks under the command of a general who, indeed, had had very little fortune.

It was two years before that same division, reformed by now, saw action again. It fought at Alamein under Montgomery and from then onwards was always at the forefront of the battle – until finally it had its revenge for the defeat at St Valery, when it helped materially to bring about the mass surrender of the one-time General (now Marshal) Rommel's vaunted *Afrika Korps* in Tunisia.

But, throughout the North African campaign, the 51st Division had seemed to have a chip on its shoulder. It had not always taken kindly to orders it didn't like and it was always seeking publicity for itself, almost in an American kind of manner. Wherever it went, it daubed everything it passed and everything it captured with the huge red letters of the divisional insignia "HD" (standing for Highland Division); as a result the Jocks became known among the other Eighth Army formations as the "Highway Decorators".

Montgomery, however, had thought so highly of the "Highway Decorators" that he had taken them with him back to England for the great invasion of Normandy. But there to its chagrin and perhaps to the delight of some of its critics, the 51st had fallen down badly. It had not shown the verve and dash it had displayed in Africa.

One officer posted to it for the first time, Major Brodie, who was to be wounded with the 51st three times before he was finished, felt constrained to tell his infantrymen before his first attack: "I was only too well aware that the Division had surrendered in 1940 and there was a tendency to make out this was a heroic act ... Somehow the newspapers had given the impression that to throw oneself on the mercy of the enemy was nothing to be ashamed of ... So I told them that, while I would not hesitate to shoot anyone who ran away, I expected them to shoot me or any officer or NCO who ordered them to pack in."[3] The result was that two of his stretcher-bearers fled, never to be seen again.

As a result of their lack of dash in Normandy, the divisional commander was replaced by one of the original "Highway Decorators" from 1940, General Thomas Rennie. He had jumped the long column of prisoners heading for the Reich and had made his way back to England via Spain. In Africa he had been wounded, and then he had been wounded again bringing the 3rd Infantry Division ashore on D-Day. Now he returned, his arm still in a sling, to take over his old division, a gentle man disdaining the red cap of the general staff, preferring the battered bonnet and red hackle of his old regiment, the Black Watch. It was he who would lead the "Highway Decorators" on their assault across the Rhine at Rees. And once again he would be wounded – only this time, fatally.

Boastfully they called themselves "Hell's Last Issue", a play on their official name, the Highland Light Infantry of Canada. Some twenty-five per cent of them had been born in the United Kingdom and most of the rest were of Scots descent, though there were a surprisingly large number of "Scots" among them with *German* names. Some of them had arrived in England over five years before and had sat there doing little but train, wine and wench until they were sent off to the great slaughter of Dieppe in 1942.

Their losses had been made up and in June 1944 they had attacked across the beaches of Normandy, determined to pay the Germans back for that terrible blood-letting at Dieppe. Again they had paid the butcher's bill to the full and in Normandy the 1st Battalion of the HLI had been virtually wiped out. Again their ranks had been filled out with reinforcements, but with difficulty; for the supply of manpower was running out. All men fighting overseas in Canada's Army were volunteers and there were many enough at home who had no wish to die for the "good old Maple Leaf" by volunteering.

In February 1945 they had slogged through the bitter battles of the Reichswald, facing not only the flower of the German Army, the paratroopers, but also sleet, snow and sodden fields, fighting on little islands of dry land among the floods, nicknaming themselves the "Water Rats" (a pun on Montgomery's "Desert Rats") because of the conditions under which they laboured.

On March 8th, just before they went into the last battle of the campaign, the war diary of the Highland Light Infantry recorded: "Weather: dull. Visibility: limited. Morale: poor – coys [companys] have taken heavy casualties and are all far below strength. Officer and NCO casualties were heavy."[4]

Brought up to full strength once more, however, they had now been given the "honour" of representing Canada at the great crossing. Someone at Canadian Army HQ had asked for representation on the Rhine, so the HLI were being attached to their fellow Jocks of the 51st Highland Division for the assault on Rees. It is doubtful whether the Canadians were appreciative of that "honour", but as their war diary recorded on the day: "Weather: clear, warm. Vis: unlimited" – and then finally, with that typical resilience of the Canadian infantryman, and especially of the HLI which boasted it had never lost a prisoner to the enemy throughout the whole long bitter campaign, "*Morale: 100 per cent!*"

"Hell's Last Issue" wouldn't let Dempsey down!

The third "Jock" formation which would take part in the assault, the 15th Scottish Division, with its rampant red lion of Scotland insignia, was a far less flamboyant unit than the "Highway Decorators" or "Hell's Last Issue". The 15th had not gone to France back in 1939. Most of the war it had spent back in Scotland in training. Nor had it been employed in the D-Day landings. To the unschooled observer it seemed a unit without any real character.

But the 15th Scottish had been a tough, hard-fighting outfit right from the start, without any of the temperamental characteristics of the other two Jock units. In its first major action it had clashed with the redoubtable "babies" of Panzermeyer's 12th SS Panzer Division, *Die Hitlerjugend*. Like the men of the 15th Scottish these eighteen- and nineteen-year-olds of the SS were going into their first action. But unlike the Scots they had been trained by officers and NCOs of the 1st

SS, *die Leibstandarte Adolf Hitler*, hardened and brutalized by their years of hard fighting in Russia. The Scots had made their mistakes and had suffered heavily for their greenness; but in the end they had triumphed and pushed on to make their first assault crossing of a great river, the Seine. By the time the war was over they would be the only Allied division to have made the three great river assaults of the war: the Seine, the Rhine and the Elbe.

Now they had just come out of the Reichswald, where they had fought and suffered for nearly six weeks in some of the worst fighting of the war. In their rifle companies, there had been an almost complete turnover of personnel due to the severe casualties. The "old sweats" of 1944 had long vanished – dead, wounded or prisoner. The "men" who would assault the Rhine were teenagers, straight from the reinforcement-holding units in Belgium or even from the training depots in the United Kingdom, leavened by a handful of older men bearing the gold wound stripes won months before in the battles of Normandy. But they would give a good account of themselves, all the same, these bandy-legged, cocky, undersized youths from the slums of Glasgow and Edinburgh. The 15th had not failed to take an objective yet in nine long months of combat; they wouldn't fail now.

The last of the British units that would attack across the Rhine below the town of Wesel – due to be "popped" first by "Bert" Harris – was the 1st Commando Brigade, the most experienced assault unit of all. For some of its members had returned to the coast of Europe to strike back and terrorize the enemy in those dark days of defeat in 1940, when many in Britain were thinking gloomily that there was no hope and that the only way out was surrender.

At dawn on June 6th, 1944, the survivors of those years of raiding the length of Europe from Norway to Southern France, strengthened now to the size of a brigade, hit the coast of France. Under their legendary leader Lord Lovat – with his personal piper and private army, the Lovat Scouts – the Commandos, laden with huge rucksacks and carrying only hand weapons, had battled against Tigers and Panthers to link up with their comrades of the 6th British Airborne Division.

On D-Ten Lord Lovat had been wounded severely in the back. As he lay on his stretcher waiting to be evacuated he looked up at Colonel Mills-Roberts, his second in-command, and gasped: "Take over the Brigade . . . and whatever happens . . . *not a foot back!*"[5]

Mills-Roberts, big, tough and one of the founder-members of the Commandos, promised he wouldn't yield a foot – and he kept his promise. For eighty-three long days the 1st Commando fought solidly in France, losing half its effectives dead or wounded, but it never relinquished a foot of ground it captured. In the end, however, it was so weary and punch drunk that when the survivors were finally allowed to sleep in the beds of a hastily evacuated German military hospital, they collapsed exhausted among waste-bins filled with gory blood-caked limbs amputated from wounded German soldiers – and didn't even notice!

In January 1945, Mills-Roberts – now a Brigadier – had brought his Commandos back to Europe for another long stint of combat, which would end this time with the total defeat of the enemy on the Baltic coast. The black days of "raiding" were at last over. This time the men of the green beret were going in for the kill.

Thus they waited then for the signal to go, the veterans and the reinforcements who still hadn't "got their knees brown" as the veterans jeered. By now their khaki battledress was shabby and wrinkled and stained, the pockets bulging with field dressings, tinned emergency rations of hard bitter chocolate, grenades and spare clips of bullets. On their backs they wore their "small packs", stuffed with ground sheet, spare socks and underpants, plus a tin perhaps of "armoured pig" (spam) or "armoured cow" (corned beef), and hanging from the buckle the inevitable battered brown or white enamel mug for tea. Without their "char" and their "coffin nails", the seven cigarettes issued to them daily while in the line, they would go nowhere.

To a casual observer watching them as they moved forward to the great attack they might have appeared more like a group of farmers with their weatherbeaten ruddy faces, leather jerkins, camouflage scarves wrapped round their necks, and their good humoured stoicism at the great loads of equipment, picks and shovels which they carried on their skinny shoulders. But they were British soldiers: British soldiers who believed that they were moving into an attack which would win the war after six long bitter years.

They were wrong, those young men of 1945. Over five thousand of them would be killed and wounded on the Rhine,[6] their sacrifice in vain. For their victory would be pointless. The overweening personal ambition of the American generals further upstream would see to that. This March Montgomery would finally "bounce" the Rhine; and it would mean nothing, absolutely nothing at all.

FIVE

On March 20th General Patton's units were moving into position all along the Rhine. His 90th Infantry Divison was closing in on Mainz. The 5th Infantry was surging forward through the wine-growing areas of the Rhineland-Palatinate, heading from the foothills to the river itself. The 11th Armored was completing its second drive for the Rhine, heading for Worms, the city where Luther had made his defiant stand nearly five hundred years before.

For three days now Patton had been flying from headquarters to headquarters, cajoling, threatening, pleading with his corps and divisional commanders. He wanted speed and yet more speed from his exhausted units. They had to reach the Rhine before Montgomery.

Three days before, Eisenhower had told him: "George, you are not only a good general, you are a *lucky* general – and as you will remember, in a general, Napoleon prized luck above skill."

"Well," Patton had laughed, "that is the first compliment you have paid me since we served together."[1]

Later Patton had told his puzzled Chief-of-Staff, who was wondering why Eisenhower had paid him and the Third Army such a compliment: "Before long Ike will be running for President. Third Army represents a lot of votes." Then, seeing the half-incredulous smiles on the faces of the men around him, he had added: "You think I'm joking? I'm not. Just wait and see."[2]

Realizing that the war no longer counted even for "Ike" and that personal glory and prestige were now all-important, Patton redoubled his efforts to get across the Rhine before Montgomery.

At ten o'clock that morning, March 20th, Patton set off in two cubs to visit General Eddy's XII Corps Headquarters to finalize his plans for the assault. Patton disdained fighter cover. "It's all right for Ike if he wants it," he barked at Colonel Codman, the former fighter-pilot who was his aide, "but I'll be goddamned if I'm going to waste gas and fighter-pilot hours protecting a couple of cubs!"[3]

But at this late stage of the war, his staff was not risking the Old Man's life. Half way to Eddy's HQ at the Hunsruck village of Simmern, Patton's spotter plane was buzzed by a fighter-plane travelling at a tremendous speed and flown by none other than General Weyland, head of the TAC Air Force. Patton relented. "When the air cover is *that* high class," he said, "I guess I can't complain."

Arriving at Eddy's HQ he was his usual brisk self. He faced the pudgy, bespectacled Corps Commander, who had been hiding his high blood pressure for months to avoid being sent home sick, and snapped: "We've got to get a bridgehead at once. Every day we save means the saving of hundreds of American lives."

Whether Eddy believed Patton's feigned concern for his men is not recorded. It is recorded, however, that he did not much like Patton's haste. He frowned and protested: "But General – I am not ready yet."

"What are you waiting for Matt?" Patton cried. "We can take the river on the run. I want you to cross the river at Oppenheim tomorrow." He indicated the little riverside town on the map, some fifteen miles south of Mainz.

"Just give us another day," Eddy appealed.

"No!" Patton cried, waving his arms angrily.

But Eddy stood his ground, jutting out his jaw aggressively, his blood pressure rising dangerously. Patton stormed out in a huff.

Eddy remembered, however, that Patton had threatened to sack him once before, back in the black days of the autumn of 1944, during the long siege of Metz. Once the Third Army Commander had left, he called the commander of his most experienced infantry division, General Leroy "Red" Irwin of the 5th. "You've got to get across, Red", Eddy said miserably. "Georgie's been tramping up and down and yelling at us."[4] And that was that.

Back in February 1943 Brigadier Irwin, as he then was, artillery commander of the 9th US Infantry Division, had helped to save the day at the disastrous battle of the Kasserine Pass in North Africa; after an eight-hundred-mile march he'd turned up in the British positions with his guns and helped the British to stave off Rommel's final attack. Then the Americans had suffered their first major defeat of the war and Alexander, the British Commander, had written to London that his chief concern was "the poor fighting value of the Americans". The Kasserine débâcle had first brought Patton into prominence – and perhaps helped to fuel his latent anglophobia.

But by March 1945 "Red" Irwin was a divisional commander and Patton, the former corps commander, led a whole army of men whose fighting value was no longer in doubt. Indeed, Irwin's 5th Infantry Division possessed a record second to none, having conquered *twenty-two* rivers held by the enemy in France, Belgium and Germany!

So, despite Eddy's misgivings, Irwin was quite optimistic that – given a little time – he could carry out Patton's plan. In essence, this plan consisted of the 90th Infantry Division making a feint near the city of Mainz, while the 5th, under cover of smoke, assaulted the river at Nierstein and Oppenheim; this, as Patton with his sense of history undoubtedly knew, was where Napoleon himself had once crossed.

Some 7,500 US engineers were alerted. Great convoys of bridging equipment began to roll towards the river from Lorraine, where they had been carefully maintained for this moment since the previous autumn. Thirteen battalions of artillery prepared to cover the crossing. And yet, even as the advance began, Irwin had doubts, for he was realist enough to know that the task was really too big for him. Time was too short even for his experienced division to do more than simply cross the river. As he protested to Eddy, it would be impossible to make "a well-planned and ordered crossing" by the night of the 22nd, the deadline set by Patton, if he were going to beat Montgomery. On the other hand, Irwin added, he would be able to "get some sort of bridgehead".

But this was all "Georgie" wanted, Eddy told him; for he already knew that Patton's chief reason for making the Rhine crossing was, as the official US Army history of World War Two puts it, "in order to beat Field-Marshal Montgomery across the river".[5]

While Irwin got on with his fevered planning for the crossing, Patton returned the compliment that General Weyland had paid him the previous day. "I'm going to run up and visit the 80th and the 10th Armoured and also take a look around in the direction of Ludwigshafen and Mannheim. Want to come along and see how the other half lives?" he asked.[6] The airman did.

As Codman reported later: "General Weyland really got an eyeful. The smashed-up towns and villages from whose remaining window frames hung sheets, pillow-cases, anything white betokening surrender à la Sicilian. The stunned silent inhabitants going sullenly about their business amidst the rubble. Higher headquarters kept issuing warnings of Werewolves and last-ditch stands, but so far the German populace had given little trouble. Now and then a village [remained] completely intact, by-passed, presumably, by our headlong advance."

As Patton commented cynically: "Of course we may have to come back here and create another Third Army memorial but for the moment they seem to get the point!"

But even Patton was awed when they came across what was left of a German horse-drawn supply column, ambushed the previous day by some of his armour ten miles from the wine-town of Neustadt. "Cannoned, machine-gunned, or simply pushed over the edge," as Codman described it, "hundreds of splintered vehicles, dead horses and Germans literally filled the gully below."

For a time Patton viewed the scene in silence. Finally he spoke. "That", he said in awed tones, "is the greatest scene of carnage I have ever witnessed. Let's go home ..."[7] That day even Patton had had enough.

"We were beat, just plain beat," Sergeant Pleasant of the 5th Division recalled later. "We'd been on the go ever since the assault crossing of the Sauer in late January. Then had come the Kyll and after that the Moselle. In the trucks and out of the trucks, day after day, week after week. I swear that most of the guys were out on their feet, sleep-walkers most of the time."[8]

Lieutenant Max Gissen of the 26th Infantry Division was equally unenthusiastic about what was to come. As he recalled after the war: "There were commanders who couldn't wait to be committed [to the Rhine crossing] and our own first colonel was one. But the men and junior officers? Nonsense! Everyone was exhausted by the time we reached the Rhine. We had suffered heavy casualties the preceding week and nothing would have pleased us better than a longish leave (say, about a year) in Paris or Biarritz or even what was left of St Lô."[9]

But if the men were exhausted and not a little pessimistic about what was waiting for them on the other side of the Rhine, the planners were full of energy and enthusiasm. Back at Patton's HQ one of his senior officers, Brigadier-General E. W. Williams, chief of the

1 The Bridge at Arnhem. At the northern end German vehicles litter the road, testimony to the bitter defence of the 1st Airborne Division. (*IWM*)

2 German troops stalk members of the Airborne Forces around Arnhem. (*IWM*)

3 Three airborne soldiers are marched into captivity after the débâcle of Market Garden. (*IWM*)

4 Some of the few lucky survivors from Arnhem who crossed the river and escaped captivity. (*IWM*)

5 Paris 1944, General de Gaulle smokes as General Leclerc, Commander 2nd French Armoured Division explains the entry into the city. It was De Gaulle who demanded of Leclerc that he should take Strasbourg even if he had to disobey his American superiors. (*IWM*)

6 Two Sherman tanks are held up by shell fire outside Cologne Cathedral as they attempt to capture the Hohenzollern Bridge. The tankman on the right has just been severely wounded. (*US Signal Corps*)

7 Too late! The Hohenzollern Bridge lies wrecked in the Rhine after being destroyed by the retreating Germans. (*Robert Hunt Picture Library*)

8 Cliffs rise above the Remagen Bridge, captured March 7th 1945 by the Ninth Armored Division of the First U.S. Army. (*US Signal Corps*)

9 An American soldier studies the Remagen Bridge from the east bank of the Rhine. (*Robert Hunt Picture Library*)

10 The story of the 'Most Famous Bridge in the World' is taped for posterity. (*Robert Hunt Picture Library*)

11 A pontoon bridge at Remagen. First U.S. Army Engineers quickly erected the bridge to speed the creation of an adequate bridgehead on the east bank of the Rhine. (*Robert Hunt Picture Library*)

12 On March 17th, after numerous attempts (including V2 missiles fired at it) to destroy it, the bridge at Remagen finally collapses into the Rhine. (*Robert Hunt Picture Library*)

13 Enemy fire forces these troops of the Third U.S. Army to cower as they cross the Rhine at Oberwesel on the 22nd March. (*US Signal Corps*)

14 The airborne armada gathers for take off. Halifax towing aircraft are lined up beside Hamilcar gliders. (*IWM*)

15 U.S. Paras about to board their Dakotas for their combat drop. (*IWM*)

16 Towing ropes lie coiled in readiness for take-off. C46 and C47 transport planes await the order to go. (*Robert Hunt Picture Library*)

17 A transport plane, with glider in tow, lifts off to join the biggest airborne offensive of the war. More than 1,500 aircraft took part. (*IWM*)

18 Hundreds of paras and their supplies over the Rees-Wesel dropping zone, 24th March 1945. (*Robert Hunt Picture Library*)

19 Some of the 40,000 airborne troops did not reach the ground. A member of 'Raff's Ruffians' of the 507th Parachute Infantry Regiment hangs from a tree in the vicinity of Wesel. (*Robert Hunt Picture Library*)

20 Hamilcar gliders having off-loaded their men and vehicles lie deserted near Hamminkeln on the east bank of the Rhine. (*IWM*)

21 British glider troops take cover next to their smashed transport which broke up on landing in enemy territory. (*Robert Hunt Picture Library*)

22 After capturing two German soldiers, these British airborne troops prepare to dash into burning Hamminkeln. (*IWM*)

23 Rivals on the Rhine. left to right: Lieutenant-General Courtney H. Hodges of the First Army, Lieutenant-General Omar N. Bradley and Lieutenant-General George S. Patton of the Third Army. (*IWM*)

24 Like some 18th century General, Winston Churchill surveys the battlefield from a convenient hilltop. On his left his personal assistant, Commander Thompson explains the lie of the land, while Field Marshal Sir Alan Brooke searches for enemy activity. (*IWM*)

25 Combat engineers of the U.S. Army prepare for the bridging of the Rhine. A transporter brings rubber pontoon floats up to the front line. (*IWM*)

26 The town of Wesel on the east bank of the Rhine suffered one of the heaviest aerial and artillery bombardments of the war. (*IWM*)

27 As dawn breaks British troops board the assault boats in which they will cross the Rhine on the 24th March. (*IWM*)

28 U.S. troops storm the German town of St Goer on 26th March. (*Robert Hunt Picture Library*)

29 The 15th Scottish Division makes a safe landing on the east bank of the Rhine, 24th March. (*IWM*)

30 Under fire, these members of the Seventh U.S. Army leave their assault boat on the enemy held east bank near Frankenthal, 26th March 1945. (*Robert Hunt Picture Library*)

31 Bombers fly over elements of the Ninth U.S. Army as they consolidate the crossing of the Rhine. (*Robert Hunt Picture Library*)

32 On the far side of the Rhine supplies were quickly amassed. A raft carries an anti-aircraft gun across to protect the bridgehead. (*Robert Hunt Picture Library*)

33 At a number of crossing points Allied troops were met by the frightened old men of the Volksstrum (German Home Guard). (*IWM*)

34 Tanks link up with the Airborne forces after the crossings. In the background a group of German prisoners wait by an abandoned glider. (*IWM*)

35 General Horrocks talks to the Field Commanders of the 51st Highland Division in the ruined town of Rees. (*IWM*)

36 The streets of Arnhem echo to the sound of fighting once again as British troops retake the town on 14th April. (*IWM*)

37 The only monument to the crossing of the Rhine. This stone erected by the French, commemorates the efforts of the soldiers of the Regiment de Tirailleurs Algeriens. (*Author's collection*)

Third Army's artillery, came up with what he thought was a brilliant idea: he would concentrate all the artillery's spotter planes and use them to take infantry across the Rhine. Each of the little planes could carry two infantrymen, so in the space of ninety minutes his planes could ferry across a whole battalion of infantry.

Patton jumped at the idea, not because of its military importance but because it would make fun of Montgomery's great airborne drop of two whole parachute divisions. Thus was born the "Third Army Troop Carrier Command", as it was proudly called.[10]

On March 22nd, Patton received one of those cables which American generals loved to send to each other at moments of triumph. This one came from General Gerow, Commander of the US Fifteenth Army. It read: "Congratulations on your brilliant surrounding and capture of three armies, one of them American" – the dig was at the US Seventh Army. The cable put Patton in a high good humour. He decided it was time to go, whether Eddy and his 5th Infantry Division were ready or not.

"What are we waiting for?" he exclaimed. He gave the signal for the 5th to attack. Thus it was that without air or artillery support, without airborne troops landing behind enemy lines, without even complete authority to do so, General George S. Patton launched his attack on the Rhine.

It was a warm moonlit night as the infantry of the 11th Infantry crept to their boats at the two riverside villages of Nierstein and Oppenheim. Here the Rhine varied in width between 800 and 1,200 feet and the men in the first wave, who would paddle themselves across, knew that they would take at least five minutes to cross. If the Germans spotted them they would be in trouble, serious trouble; and those of them who had assault-crossed the River Sauer the previous January remembered too well the casualties they had taken that icy, bloody night.

Behind them the engineers and tankers waited tensely. Once the initial force was across, the engineers would begin building a pontoon bridge, so that the tanks of the 4th Armored could cross and commence the breakout.

On the heights above the river, senior officers crouched tensely with their binoculars focused on the silver-glowing land on the opposite side, waiting for the first scarlet flash of fire. Below them the troops had begun to emerge from the barge harbour that had hidden their assault boats, moving out onto the river itself. The strained silence was broken only by the splash of the soldiers' paddles ...

Nothing happened. The Germans had not spotted them. Five minutes later Lieutenant Irven Jacobs commanding Company K and eight of his men had reached the other side of the Rhine. Then, clambering up the muddy reed-covered bank, they came upon seven very surprised Germans who immediately surrendered.

Patton had crossed at Nierstein, its only claim to fame thus far its local wine, without having to fire a single shot. He had done it at last – he had crossed the Rhine!

A few hundred yards upstream, just below the hilltop village of Oppenheim, Companies A and B of the 11th Infantry were not so fortunate. Their assault boats had just reached mid-stream when German machine guns opened up on them. For an instant some of the paddlers hesitated as the bullets zipped lethally across the water. But then they started to paddle once more, going all-out for there was no turning back. Now they headed straight into the enemy fire.

Here and there boats overturned, casting their panicked infantrymen laden with heavy equipment into the Rhine. Others simply drifted, their crews either dead or dying, drowning in their own blood. But the rest continued, springing ashore, weapons at the ready, heading straight for the gunners.

Half an hour later it was all over. The German defenders were either dead or running for their lives. Now the rest of the 11th Infantry Regiment could cross.

By daylight the second regiment of the 5th Infantry Division was across too, braving the German shelling *and* the first German air attack, as twelve fighters zoomed in low over the Rhine to drop their bombs on the bridgehead. Now the leading infantry started to fan out as the German resistance began to thicken, being pinned down here and there until their squad leaders rallied them and, employing "walking death" (intense marching fire), got them moving again.

A hundred or so Germans launched a determined counter-attack on the Division's 3rd Battalion; but as it grew lighter to the east and the Americans could spot the German positions more clearly, they began to surrender en masse. The Division's 10th Battalion also ran into trouble, but managed to overcome it.

So, by the time General Patton was awakened for breakfast by his old and trusty coloured servant, his men were firmly entrenched on the other side of the Rhine and the construction of the pontoon bridge was well under way, despite the ever-increasing German air attacks. By the end of that day the Third Army would claim to have shot down thirty-three planes over the bridgehead.

Bradley was just finishing his second cup of breakfast coffee at his HQ in Namur when a jubilant Patton called him, trying to suppress the glee he felt as he heard Bradley's familiar voice at the other end. "Brad," he said, "don't tell anyone, but I'm across."

"Across what, George?" Bradley asked in surprise.

"The Rhine! And you can tell the world the Third Army made it before Monty!"

Bradley nearly choked on his coffee. "Well I'll be damned!" he spluttered. "You mean across the Rhine?"

"Sure!" Patton replied. "I sneaked a division across last night. But there are so few Krauts around there they don't know it yet. So don't make any announcement. We'll keep it a secret till we see how it goes, eh?"

Bradley agreed. But soon the Army Commander changed his mind. Later that same day an almost hysterical Patton called him again to tell him: "Brad, for God's sake tell the world we're across! We knocked down thirty-three Krauts today when they came after our pontoon bridges. I want the world to know the Third Army made it before Montgomery starts across."[11]

Bradley's announcement was, as the official US history puts it, "aimed at needling Field-Marshal Montgomery". Bradley's HQ stated at the morning briefing: "Without benefit of aerial bombardment, ground smoke, artillery preparation and airborne assistance, the Third Army at 2200 hours Thursday evening, 22nd March, crossed the Rhine River."[12]

One day later, as Montgomery's young men engaged in bloody battle to so little purpose now due to the events at Oppenheim, Patton reported to his Supreme Commander laconically: *"Today I pissed in the Rhine!"*[13]

PART III

Victory on the Rhine

Over the Rhine then let us go and finish off the German war as soon as possible ... And good hunting to you all on the other side!
  Field-Marshal Montgomery, March 23rd, 1945

ONE

In Italy the big, bluff Field-Marshal Kesselring was known to his soldiers as "Smiling Albert". No matter how gloomy the situation, he always seemed to be smiling and optimistic. But even Kesselring would soon have the smile wiped from his face.

For nearly two years Kesselring had fought a successful rearguard action against the Allies in Italy. Time and time again the Allies had tried to catch him off guard by launching a landing behind his front, but he never panicked; indeed, he had proved himself a past master of defensive actions, making the Allies pay a very high price for their successes at Cassino, the Hitler and Gothic Lines. He was regarded as so tough that once when he suffered a concussion after his car had collided with an artillery piece, his troops quipped that "Smiling Albert" was doing fine but the cannon had had to be scrapped!

Now with the Rhine already breached and a major attack on its whole length soon to come, Hitler summoned Kesselring from Italy to replace the ageing Field-Marshal von Rundstedt as Commander-in-Chief West. If anyone could save the day, the Führer reasoned, it would be Kesselring.

Kesselring set off in his usual brisk fashion. Introducing himself to his new staff at Command Headquarters at Ziegenberg, Hesse, and knowing that they had already heard of the supposed new wonder-weapon which would turn back the tide of war in Germany's favour, he said sardonically, "*Meine Herren*, I am the new V-3!"

In his typical outspoken fashion, however, he soon succeeded in putting up the backs of his principal subordinates. Out on a reconnaissance of the front with his Chief-of-Staff, General Westphal, who had served in the same capacity with von Rundstedt, they passed weary *landsers* streaming eastwards with their weapons and packs laden on little carts. "So this is the situation as it really is in the west," Kesselring remarked angrily. "If I'd only come three months ago!"[1]

Westphal not surprisingly felt the remark was a slur on his old Chief.

Later Kesselring also managed to irritate no less a person than Field-Marshal Model, who had gained as great a reputation for defensive tactics in Russia as Kesselring had in Italy.

"Throw the Americans back across the Rhine!" "Smiling Albert" ordered the little Marshal.

"I'll try," Model answered testily. "But I don't think my forces are sufficient."

And as that first day of command passed, even Kesselring, the notorious optimist, realized the enormity of what he was asking. As he said himself later, he "felt like a concert pianist who is asked to play a Beethoven sonata ... on an ancient, rickety and out-of-tune instrument".[2] He simply did not have the men or the resources to do what was soon to be expected of him – to stop the Allies, in particular Montgomery, on the Rhine.

Still, in his usual stubborn manner, he tried. On the afternoon of the 21st he conferred with Westphal on the state of his front. Westphal indicated the rash of red and blue crayon marks on the map. "These are the main enemy forces," he told his new chief. "According to our latest information there must be about ninety divisions in all. The places with red circles around them to the east and south of the Ruhr are the airfields and train yards which the enemy has been bombing since early morning."

Kesselring absorbed the information, trying to assess from the air attacks – obviously part of the enemy's softening-up process – what his strategy on the Lower Rhine should be. "If I calculate correctly," he said after a few moments, "We have sixty-five nominal divisions. What is their real strength?"

"About half that number."[3]

Kesselring frowned. That meant he was going to fend off ninety divisions with the equivalent of thirty-odd. It was not an enviable position for "Smiling Albert".

As yet, however, the new commander in the west did not know the calibre of those troops, especially the ones facing Montgomery on the

Rhine. They were in fact some of the best troops left in the Greater German Wehrmacht: they were the men of the First Parachute Army.

Although they belonged to famous parachute divisions such as the 7th, which had virtually conquered Holland single-handed from the air back in 1940, only a handful of them had ever jumped from a plane; they were paras in name only. Most of these youngsters in their rimless helmets and baggy camouflage suits had received only a couple of months of infantry training. But what they lacked in experience and training they made up for by their youthful enthusiasm and their complete faith in the National Socialist cause.

These young recruits or men transferred from the beaten Luftwaffe swiftly developed the *esprit de corps* that regular Wehrmacht divisions had long lost. They felt themselves worthy successors to those *fallschirmjaeger* who had fought and died at Eben Emael, Crete, Monte Cassino and the like. They even swore personal oaths to their commanders and their units, vowing to uphold their honour. In Colonel von der Heydte's regiment, for instance, every recruit raised his hand as if in a court of law and promised "*Ja, ich schwoere*" to the long harangue which stated: "I demand of every soldier the renunciation of all personal wishes. Whoever swears on the Prussian flag has no right to personal possessions. From the moment he enlists in the paratroops and comes to my regiment every soldier enters the new order of humanity and gives up everything. There is only one law henceforth for him – the law of our unit ... He must give up personal weaknesses and ambitions and realize that our battle is for the existence of the whole German nation and that no end to the war other than a German victory is conceivable."[4]

Inspired by the "old hares", as the veterans were called, these "greenbeaks" fought with dash, determination and fanaticism. Time and time again during the January and February battles across the Rhine in the Reichswald they had held out against tremendous odds, only yielding ground when ordered to by their commanders. Even their opponents respected them. Corporal Wingfield with the 7th Armored Division noted, just before one of those self-same paras shot him and put him out of action for good: "We felt quite a professional affection for these paratroops. They were infantry-trained like us to use their own initiative. They had the same system of "trench-mates". They fought cleanly and treated prisoners, wounded and dead with the same respect they expected from us. If our uniforms had been the same we would have welcomed them as kindred spirits."[5]

Indeed, as the last of the surviving paras surrendered in the city of Xanten on the west bank of the Rhine facing Wesel, the British brigadier in charge of the 43rd Infantry Division ordered his staff to stand to attention in silent salute as the defeated paras shuffled wearily past, heading for the cage.

But although these young men who were soon to defend the Lower Rhine against Montgomery were feared and respected by their enemies, they were heartily disliked by the remaining civilians on the far bank of the Rhine. Towns such as Rees, held by the 7th Para Division, were up to eighty per cent destroyed already. The years of bombing by the RAF and USAF had taken their toll. Leave men from the Wehrmacht would commonly remark that they'd be glad when their home leave was over because "It's more dangerous here than it is at the front!"

The real war for these Rhenish towns of the Lower Rhine had started on a warm September Sunday in 1944, when citizens enjoying a lazy afternoon stroll had seen the first planes carrying the 1st British Parachute Division – due to land at Arnhem on the other side of the border – come crashing down in flames. From that day on they had been in the front line. Most of the winter the locals had been subjected to forced labour, building what Gauleiter Meyer of Münster proudly called the "Westphalian Wall": a series of holes and bunkers that stretched through Westphalia to Wesel. This "Wall" was now manned by fifteen German soldiers per kilometre, with artillery cannon every three or four kilometres, flak guns for every two or 3 kilometres, plus one tank for every two kilometres. Every able-bodied man, woman and child on the other side of the Rhine was soon set to work on the other fortifications which the Party thought would stop the British and Canadians in the Reichswald. And all the while, towns such as Rees and Wesel had been subjected to day after day of heavy bombing, the RAF at night, the *Amis* during the daylight hours.

Much as the civilians might hate the "Allied air gangsters", however, they hated the Party's "golden pheasants" even more: those uniformed apes with their many decorations who had brought all this misery upon them.

Even Doctor Goebbels, the dwarf-like, club-footed Minister of Propaganda, the Reich's main advocate of defence to the last man and the last bullet, had to admit that the men and women of his native Rhineland were heartily sick of the war. On the very same day that

Montgomery would launch his great assault, Goebbels noted in his diary: "In many places the population hoisted white flags in areas occupied by the Anglo-Americans as the Gauleiters freely admit. The reason is, however, that they had no wish to lose what remained of their houses and dwellings. At the moment no one in the West talks of capitulation; but when the war reaches anyone's vincinity everyone hopes to see it blast its way over him as quickly as possible ... Among most sections of the German people faith in victory has totally vanished ... Hardly anywhere is there any hope of a happy ending to the war."

The inhabitants of Rees and Wesel and the surrounding villages were now confronted by tough young paras digging in everywhere, turning what was left of their homes and farmhouses into mini-fortresses, obviously expecting another Stalingrad; and they didn't like it.

In Rees, the bold young commander of a para battalion who wore the black and white Knight's Cross of the Iron Cross around his neck, decided to use the local hospital as his command post. The doctors protested but the para captain would not listen. In due course the hospital would be struck by a salvo of British shells, being recognized as a military installation in spite of the huge red cross on its roof, and it was burnt down. Another para officer, in a drunken moment, decided he would blow up the city's stretch of historical medieval wall along the front of the Rhine to obtain a better field of fire; he was only stopped by a senior officer at the very last moment.

In the end, the survivors of the bombing and the shelling gave in. They could do nothing with the paras. So receiving a general absolution from their priests, saying goodbye to the remaining officials who had not fled with the rest of the Party's "golden pheasants" (including the Mayor of Rees, who would be dead from shell-fire before this terrible week was over), they took to their cellars and waited. Three days later when they returned to the surface they would not recognize the lunar landscape that had once been proud medieval cities and prosperous farming villages.

"Smiling Albert" waited too. He had already guessed what Montgomery, across the river, was planning. "The enemy's air operations in a clearly limited area, bombing raids on headquarters and the smoke screening and assembly of bridging material indicated the enemy's intention to attack between Emmerich and Dinslaken,"

Kesselring later recorded. And, he added, "The cloudless spring weather gave Montgomery the opportunity for a large-scale airborne landing."

But there was little he could do until Montgomery started the attack. The great days of 1940 and 1941 with their tremendous victories for the German Army were over. Now the Commander-in-Chief West no longer *acted*; he *reacted*.

As dawn broke on Friday, March 23rd, 1945, the actors were in place; soon the drama could commence.

TWO

No one had wanted him here in the first place but he had been determined to come and see his "redcoats", as he liked to imagine them, to watch them cross the last barrier, one along which he himself had sailed in a Royal Navy torpedo-boat over a quarter of a century before. Montgomery had been horrified when he heard the news. "It just was not on," he is reported to have said; he did not want the Prime Minister "wandering about in the middle of the battle disturbing the commanders who were running it".[1]

But Churchill dug his heels in, obstinately resolved to be present at the great crossing. Alan Brooke, the CIGS, wrote to his protégé Montgomery: "If the Prime Minister is not allowed to come, you have the seeds of serious trouble ahead. When the PM gets such ideas in his head nothing will stop him." Privately he confided to his own diary: "I am not happy with this trip. He will be difficult to manage and has no business to be going. All he will do is to endanger his life unnecessarily and get in everyone's way and be a damned nuisance to everybody ... However, nothing can stop him."[2]

Montgomery gave in with poor grace. He wrote to Grigg, the Minister of War and an old friend: "I am expecting the P.M. here on the 23rd. He seems to be getting restless and querulous. Why he wants to go about in dangerous places I cannot imagine. He may quite likely get shot up. However, it is his own affair. I shall make it quite clear to him that he goes to these dangerous places against my definite advice and then leave it to him. I shall be far too busy to attend to him."[3]

Eisenhower's reaction was more practical. He told Simpson, the Ninth Army Commander, to ensure that there was plenty of Scotch, for "Winnie" was coming and "Winnie" dearly loved his Scotch.

After lunch that Friday the Prime Minister's party, including Brooke, his bodyguard, Commander "Tommy" Thompson, and his private secretary "Jock" Colville, dressed in RAF uniform, set off for the airport at Northolt. Churchill was in high good humour and had dressed himself in the uniform of his old regiment, the Fourth Hussars, which he had joined as a subaltern in 1895 and had served with in India. On their way to the airport they encountered a diversion; the road was up. Their driver was about to turn around, but Churchill waved his big cigar and insisted they should continue. As Brooke observed: "This meant lifting some of the barriers, driving on the footpath etc and on the whole probably took longer than going round. However, Winston was delighted he was exercising his authority and informed me that the King would not take such action: he was far more law-abiding."[4]

At three o'clock precisely Churchill's Dakota took off for the two-hour flight to Montgomery's battle HQ at Venlo on the German–Dutch border. Meanwhile Montgomery, dressed in an old pullover and baggy corduroy trousers, waited for the final weather report on which would depend whether or not his great force launched the attack tonight. His message to the troops had already been prepared: "The enemy possibly thinks he is safe behind this great river obstacle. We all agree that it is a great obstacle; but we will show the enemy that he is far from safe behind it." Here Montgomery resorted to the sporting images and clichés typical of his class – "the sticky wickets" and "knocking them for six" of his previous addresses to his troops. "Having crossed the Rhine we will crack about in the plains of Northern Germany, chasing the enemy from pillar to post ... Over the Rhine then let us go and finish off the German war as soon as possible ... And good hunting to you all on the other side!"[5]

His final appeal was, as usual, to God himself. "May 'The Lord mighty in battle' give us victory in this our latest undertaking as He has done in all our battles since we landed in Normandy on D-Day."

"The Lord mighty in battle" would indeed give Montgomery the victory he asked for; but there would be no "cracking about" on the plains of Northern Germany thereafter. This would be Field-Marshal Montgomery's last victory – one that led nowhere.

At three thirty that warm and sunny afternoon, as the waiting assault troops lazed on the grass awaiting their call to arms behind the cover of a nauseating smoke-screen, Montgomery made his decision. He gave the code word for the start of the great operation: *"Two if by sea."* He'd chosen, puckishly, part of the signal that had set Paul Revere galloping through the Yankee countryside in 1775 to warn the minutemen that the "redcoats" were coming; only today the bright red coats, pigtails and stocks had been replaced by dull khaki and camouflage scarves.

Shortly afterwards the Churchill party arrived to find Montgomery immensely proud of the fact that he had been able to set up his camp inside Germany at last.

As tea was served and Montgomery began to explain his plans to the Prime Minister, the entire front erupted the length of its twenty-two miles as a well orchestrated cataclysm of 3,500 field guns and 2,000 anti-tank guns and rocket projectors commenced plastering the German defenders.

After dinner, while the guns still roared and rumbled, Montgomery excused himself and retired to his caravan as was his wont; he was not letting himself be put off his early sleep by Churchill or the Germans. But Brooke and the Prime Minister were too excited to sleep. Together they walked outside in the moonlight, talking about old times and their early struggles. Churchill told Brooke that he had had to take his, Brooke's, decision that "Alex" and "Monty" could win the desert war for him on trust. But it had all worked out well. Now here they were on the Rhine. Brooke nodded his agreement. It all seemed long, long ago and he was very weary, physically and mentally. And, as they were to rise early on the following morning to watch the second phase of Montgomery's attack, the two-division-strong airborne landing, he decided they'd better get some sleep. He bade the Prime Minister goodnight and retired to his quarters. "I am now off to bed," he wrote in his diary that night. "It is hard to realize that within fifteen miles hundreds of men are engaged in death-struggles along the banks of the Rhine, whilst hundreds more are keying themselves up to stand up to one of the greatest trials of their lives. With that thought in one's mind it is not easy to lie down and sleep peacefully."[6]

The thunder of the guns continued, lighting up the whole length of river as shell after shell crashed into the German positions, the roar rising by the instant. Shots fell into the water itself, sending up huge spurts of wild white water with the sound of a giant red-hot poker being plunged in. Tracer zig-zagged lethally back and forth. Mortars howled. Rockets screeched high into the silver gloom, drawing their fiery-red trails after them. All was noise, confusion and sudden death.

"The noise was so terrific," the historian of the Lincolns recorded, "that conversation in Battalion Headquarters became almost impossible."[7] "Our targets were pre-selected and the guns lost the paint from their barrels," recollected R. G. Saunders of the 103rd Regiment Royal Artillery.[8] Captain Wilson, waiting to cross with his section of flame-throwers, remembered later: "East and west as far as I could see the night was lit with gunfire; it flickered through the trees and flashed on the underside of the clouds. The ground shook ceaselessly and now and again there was a violent continuing explosion like a pack of cards being snapped."[9]

The order was given for the assault troops to start clambering into their Buffaloes for the assault crossing. Most of them, Canadian, British and American were nervous. They told jokes "which no one would have laughed at ordinarily," Captain Wilson noted, "wandering off frequently to the latrine."[10] A sure sign of funk.

Eisenhower, who had arrived with Simpson to watch the crossing of his veteran 30th Infantry Division, noticed one young soldier looking fearful, his face pale and shiny in the flickering pink light. "How are you feeling?" asked Eisenhower, cupping his hands around his mouth to make himself heard over the ear-splitting barrage.

"General, I'm awful nervous," the boy replied, "I was wounded two months ago and just got back from the hospital yesterday. I don't feel so good."

"Well, you and I are a good pair then," Eisenhower bellowed back, "because I'm nervous too. But we've planned this attack for a long time and we've got all the planes, the guns and airborne troops we can use to smash the Germans. Maybe if we just walk along together to the river we'll be good for each other."[11] Which was how a five-star general in his fifties came to be walking around with a nervous young private on the banks of the Rhine.

And Eisenhower was not the only uneasy general on the Rhine that night. As the bombardment started to die down, General Horrocks, commander of XXX Corps, climbed to his observation post on some high ground to wait for the first reports from his 51st Division and "Hell's Last Issue" which would cross opposite Rees. "All around me were the usual noises of battle," he wrote later, "and though I could see very little except the flicker of the guns, I had a mental picture of what was going on in front of me in the hazy darkness ... I could imagine the leading Buffaloes carrying infantry of 153rd and 154th Infantry Brigades lumbering along their routes which had been taped out and lit beforehand and then lurching forward into the dark waters of the Rhine."[12]

Horrocks was also worried about General Rennie. He and Rennie had fought together many times before, but he had never seen the Scot so edgy as now. Was he fey perhaps? Did he have the Celt's sixth sense when some disaster was about to occur?

The regiment to which Rennie belonged had been started back in 1739, set up by "Our Right Trusty and Right Well-Beloved Cousin John Earl of Crawford and Lindsay" (as the Royal Decree put it): six companies of militia known as the Black Watch – "Black" because of their sombre tartans, "Watch" because they were a guard rather than a military unit. For over two centuries they had served King and Country loyally in four continents; once they had even fought the Americans. Now the same Black Watch were going to spearhead the "Highway Decorators'" drive across the Rhine, the last great battle.

At precisely nine o'clock that perfect moonlit night, their Buffaloes waddled into the river like great metal ducks. In the lead were the 7th Battalion of the Black Watch, plus the 7th Argylls, their long-standing rivals, followed by the 1st Battalion the Black Watch: all battalions with an old, old score to settle – the surrender at St Valery in June 1940.

Eagerly they surged across the broad, silvery Rhine, its far bank shrouded with smoke, the foam swirling a brilliant white at the sides of their ungainly craft. Laden down with their shell dressings, life-belts, equipment, weapons, and shovels, the men were tense but confident. Nothing would stop them.

Within two or three minutes they were landing on the opposite side, splashing and slipping as they scrambled up the bank through the lethal morse of tracer and the scarlet stab of flame piercing the darkness, while the senior officer there, Colonel Jolly of the Royal Tank Corps, planted his regiment's flag in the mud. As always the British tried to do things in style.

A Buffalo rose from the ground momentarily and reeled to a sudden stop like some stricken monster; it had run over a teller anti-tank mine. Up front, as the infantry started to spread out to secure the tiny bridgehead, there were sudden curses and screams of pain as the first men stepped on the feared schu-mines. Writhing and twisting in the mud, hugging their shattered limbs, faces ashen, they called that old sad cry: "Stretcher-bearer! ... Stretcher-bearer!"

They were across, with only a handful of casualties, and already at four minutes past nine their anxious Corps Commander General Horrocks had received the message he was waiting for: "*The Black Watch has landed safely on the far bank.*"

At ten o'clock it was the turn of the 1st Commando Brigade. War correspondent R. W. Thompson was watching as they moved out. "Never have I seen troops so magnificently confident," he wrote. "The back of the Buffalo closed. Without pause the amphibious tank roared back over the dyke and within two minutes crunched down into the Rhine. Overhead the perfect sky was filled with vast red sheaves of tracer pouring from Bofors and the harsh muttering of massed machine guns weaved incessantly under the whip-lash of the heavier guns."[13]

In one Buffalo was Corporal Cosgrave, a veteran of Normandy, who had gone hungry often enough there and was determined not to suffer the same way again. Somewhere he had "liberated" what he thought was a fat drake, which he had dubbed Hector. Currently Hector was strapped to the top of his pack and would in due course be roasted on the other side of the Rhine. Hector started to squawk with fright. He started to make the other Commandos crouched in the Buffalo nervous. "Shut the fucking thing up Corp, willyer?" they called repeatedly. In the end, Cosgrave sealed Hector's beak with tape and thus, in canard silence at least, they crossed the Rhine.

Captain Barry Pierce of the Royal Marines was the first to reach the other side. As the artillery fire lifted and the first dazed Germans started to pop up their heads, Pierce went at them. This was trench warfare, vintage 1915. Grenades hissed, tommy guns chattered at close quarters, and then the Commandos were at them with, in the parlance of that old war, "cold steel". Within five minutes the German resistance had crumbled.

The first Buffalo was hit. As it nosed its way out of control it burst into scarlet flame. The burning fuel seared the length of the deck like a gigantic blow torch. Badly wounded and burnt, Lieutenant W. A. James leapt ashore, gritting his teeth against the pain. Behind him followed a handful of signallers plus an observer officer from the mountain battery, whose guns would play such an important role in the confused fighting of these shattered Rhenish cities.

The Commandos went scurrying for cover, most of them heading for a large factory which they had selected as a rallying spot before the crossing. It turned out to be a factory for the manufacture of what is quaintly called "sanitary ware". As Corporal Cosgrave commented long afterwards: "That night more of the blokes were wounded by splinters of flying shithouses than they were by Jerry bullets!"[14] But at that moment it was considered to be a highly desirable place to be, for "Arthur Harris and Company, House Removers", as the RAF was known to the Commandos, were on their way: 250 Lancasters and Mosquitos preparing to drop 2,000 tons of high explosive on the already shattered city of Wesel. The time had come to "pop the Wesel"!

"I looked at my watch," Thompson recorded for the *Sunday Times*. "It was ten thirty to the minute. A day earlier we had been told that an important key town would be "blotted". And now, deluging down out of the sky, an appalling weight of bombs seemed to rip both town and the very earth itself to fragments, and at once a great crimson stain of smoke and flame poured up like an open wound so that the puffs of the bursting flak were crimson too and the river seemed the colour of blood."[15]

Watching the awesome spectacle from the other side, Moorehead recorded: "The Lancasters filled the air with roaring and at last the cataclysmic unbelievable shock of the strike. Great black stretches of the skyline – buildings and trees and wide acres of city parkland – simply detached themselves from the earth and mounted slowly upwards in the formation of a fountain. As the rubble reached its zenith, it suddenly filled with bursting light and a violent wind came tearing across the river."[16]

To Commando Major Bartholomew, reeling and gasping from the shock of that tremendous bombardment, "It seemed as if more than mortal powers had been unleashed."[17]

That night Wesel died.

But to the tough young men in their green berets – they disdained helmets that night – the Germans deserved all they got. Fifteen minutes after the last of the bombers had disappeared, leaving behind them an echoing silence broken only by the crackle of the flames, No. 1 Commando Brigade made its first contact with the anxiously waiting staff on the west bank of the Rhine. To the tense staff officers the voice on the radio set seemed "literally to purr" as it sent the triumphant signal: *"Noisy blighters aren't they."* (The unknown commando meant "Arthur Harris and Company House Removers".) *"We have taken the position . . . and have met no trouble."*[18]

The listening men, faces pale in the flaring, hissing light of the lantern, heaved a collective sigh of relief. The 1st Commando was across too. Now Montgomery had a bridgehead at both ends of his front. All was going well.

THREE

The "Old Man" seemed to tremble at every limb. He stank, too, for he swallowed some sixty tablets a day and broke wind constantly. Once he had been master of the greatest empire Europe had seen since the days of Rome, lording it over some three hundred million people. He had boasted his empire would last a thousand years; yet already after a mere twelve years it was falling apart. But as he sat there trembling, surrounded by his handful of courtiers, he did not yet realize that this Saturday's events marked the end.

For nearly thirty minutes Hitler and his followers had discussed the Rhine situation and the problem of reinforcements for the Western Front. Patton's crossing of the Rhine at Oppenheim two days before was what most vexed him. "I really consider the second bridgehead, the bridgehead at Oppenheim, the greatest danger," he quavered. Still there was the problem of the long-standing bridgehead at Remagen to be taken into consideration. Hodges was pushing hard to break out there and German reinforcements were badly needed to bolster up the sagging front in the Westerwald.

One of Hitler's toadies, General Burgdorf, suggested he might find his reinforcements in the Indian Legion, made up of renegades from the Commonwealth Armies, culled from German prisoner-of-war camps.

"The Indian Legion is a joke," Hitler said with some animation. "There are Indians who can't kill a louse and would rather let themselves be eaten up . . . I think if we use Indians to turn prayer wheels or something like that they'd be the most indefatigable soldiers in the world. But to use them in a real death struggle is ridiculous."[1]

It was just about then a liaison officer, flushed and excited, burst into the conference to bring his tidings of woe. "*Mein Führer*," he snapped. "Army Group H reported at three o'clock that the enemy has moved up for the attack one and half kilometres south of Wesel and near Mehrum. The strength and nature of this attack has not yet been reported."

Immediately the little band of thugs, soldiers and courtiers began discussing the situation at Wesel until one of them reminded Hitler that there were not enough reinforcements to stop Patton at Oppenheim. There were only five self-propelled guns available and they wouldn't be ready for another day.

"Actually they were meant for the upper bridgehead," Hitler objected.

"Yes, *mein Führer*," agreed Borgmann, the liaison officer. "For the 512th Battalion at Remagen."

"When do they leave?"

"They'll be ready today or tomorrow," Borgmann answered. "They can probably move tomorrow night."

"Then we'll take that up again tomorrow," Hitler decided. Now he started to muse out loud how soon a group of "sixteen or seventeen Tigers" could be repaired and sent to the front. "That would be very important."

Thus the "Old Man" who had once ruled the destiny of Europe played with handfuls of tanks. It was three thirty on the morning of Saturday, March 24th. The end of the Third Reich was not far away.

But if Hitler had retreated into a dream world, "Smiling Albert" Kesselring still had his feet firmly on the ground and he was determined to contain this new threat to his Rhine Line. In Holland he had already alerted his first reserve, the 116th Panzer Division – "the Greyhounds" as they called themselves – a veteran division which would swing right behind the Rhine front and stop any further landings on the right flank of the Commandos. On the left flank he ordered General Raspe's 15th Panzer Grenadiers into action against the "Highway Decorators", trying to establish their positions near Rees. Raspe, burly and red-faced, a veteran of the Desert where he had fought against the 51st before, immediately sent his tanks and armoured personnel carriers into action for a bold counter stroke. Soon they would make the "Highway Decorators" pay for their surprise crossing and bring tragedy to that unlucky 51st Highland Division.[2]

Now it was the turn of the 15th Scottish Division to cross. Wynford Vaughan Thomas of the BBC went with them; his last glimpse of the Rhine had been at that abortive French crossing of the previous November. It was hardly an enjoyable experience for him but it did have its funny moments.

"Racing for that hell on the other side ... Now we're utterly alone it seems ... right out in the midst of this whirling stream ... waiting all the time for the enemy to open up... waiting all the time for them to spot us as we lie helpless ..." But the BBC man and the Jocks were not spotted, and he recorded for his BBC listeners: "We were across untouched. Well, there was an immense feeling of relief and excitement throughout our little party."

The CO of the assault party nodded to his piper. The historic moment obviously had to be celebrated in true Scottish fashion; so, with due ceremony, the piper raised his pipes to his lips and blew hard.

Nothing happened.

He tried again. Still nothing and then an agonizing wail. As Thomas remarked: "If ever a man was near to tears it was our piper." It was his great moment and he had failed. Now the Scot cried in despair: "Ma pipes, mon ... *they'll nae play!*"[3]

Now the men of the 15th Scottish started to push forward, past a lone cowshed in a sodden pasture towards the village of Bislich, a handful of low cottages grouped round a tiny church.

Watching from the other bank, novelist John Prebble noted: "The air was full of noise. Beyond the avenue of trees that led to the old ferry, elms that were now splintered and defoliated, the guns were firing regularly. The air about ... grinded with the noise of vehicles, the shouting of men." And yet, Prebble went on, he felt a sudden surge of intense joy: "My happiness felt no limits. It was, in essence, a sensual happiness, a pleasure derived from mere physical excitement, but also in my blood throbbed something of the urgency of the day, an Army swarming across a river."[4]

But to the left of the triumphant 15th Scottish Division, the initial elation of the men of the 51st had vanished. They were beginning to run into trouble as the paratroopers, aided by the tanks, started to hit back.

The 1st Battalion of the Black Watch which had come in the second wave had now commenced moving out of the bridgehead towards the villages of Speldrop and Klein-Esserden, where General Erdmann's *fallschirmjager* of the 7th Airborne Division were well dug in. At Klein-Esserden in particular, Erdmann's men were buried deep in the cellars and protected by extensive minefields in the flat sodden fields all around.

Led by Major Richard Boyle, who had left a safe staff job for the honour of crossing the Rhine in battle, the lead company started forward, the Jocks holding their rifles across their chests in the high port, advancing against machine-gun fire like weary farm-labourers trudging home after a hard day's work.

Years before, in hiding after the Crete débâcle, Boyle had written home to his soldier father: "Means of escape are practically nil as the Germans have got hold of all the motor and sailing boats. So I shall have to spend the winter in the island ... It is better than being in a prison camp."[5] Somehow he had managed to escape – and arrived back in Egypt completely naked! Thereafter he had survived half a score of other adventures. Now, in the moment of victory, Boyle's luck ran out. He was ripped apart by the sheer volume of German fire. His men fell back as the Germans counter-attacked with tanks and self-propelled guns.

It was no different at the next village of Speldrop. Here the Germans were pressing so hard that the lead company feared it would be overrun. Hastily Colonel Hopwood ordered his men to withdraw to a local factory which could be more easily defended; but in the confusion one of his platoons was cut off. Nineteen-year old Second-Lieutenant Robert Henderson volunteered to try to get in touch with it. The Colonel hesitated, but the subaltern was adamant; and in the end the Colonel gave in.

Together with a Bren-gunner, Henderson crawled down a ditch towards the main road. A German machine gun opened up. The Bren-gunner screamed, threw up his hands wildly, and fell to the ground dead. Henderson yelped with pain as his revolver was shot from his hand. But still the teenager did not give up. He whipped the shovel he was carrying from his back and, with the same wild fury that had animated his Gaelic ancestors, rushed forward at the machine-gun post, wielding the shovel like they might have done their claymores. The German went reeling back, his skull smashed in. Henderson joined the cut-off platoon and would fight with them for two long days to come before they were finally relieved. One month later he was rewarded for his efforts that day; he received a decoration that is usually reserved for colonels twice his age – the

Distinguished Service Order. Few officers had ever received the award so young.

But slowly the "Highway Decorators" were bogging down, running into trouble virtually everywhere as they tried to take the key town of Rees. In spite of the reports that large numbers of German soldiers were surrendering elsewhere, the 51st Highland Division reported back to Corps that the "enemy was fighting harder than at any time since Normandy". As the Corps Commander Horrocks would write later, in praise of those hard-bitten enemy paras defending Rees and area: "It says a lot for the morale of those German parachute and panzer troops that with chaos, disorganization and disillusionment all around them, they should still be resisting so stubbornly."[6]

Horrocks gave the order for the Canadians to start crossing; the "Highway Decorators" might well need their support as it grew light. At four that morning they started to cross. One of them, Private Malcolm Buchanan of the "Hell's Last Issue", later recorded his memories of that moment. "The whole sky seemed to light up as the guns commenced firing ... On coming down to get into the boats ... I almost ran over a newsreel cameraman who was taking pictures of the men as they came down the bank. As number one on the Bren my position was in the front of the boat. At that point the river looked awfully wide, foggy and lonesome. I asked the operator of our boat why we had been singled out to have our picture taken. 'You,' he said, 'will be the first man to hit the shore. How do you like *that?*'

"Well, to tell the truth the answer kind of stunned me. Here I was loaded down like a horse. Boy, I thought, we'll never make it across."[7]

But Buchanan made it. While the shells screamed overhead, the man at the engine of the assault boat let her rip full out. All the same, although it was only a four-minute crossing, it "seemed like an hour" to Private Buchanan.

Behind him came Corporal Sam Dearden of the same Brigade, in charge of a carrier and a six-pounder anti-tank gun. Now his officer asked him to man a 20 mm cannon fixed to the assault craft, advising him at the same time to wear his steel helmet.

Dearden shrugged. "From the size of the shells falling nearby," he commented later, "it would be of little use."

Somehow they got across, only to run straight into trouble. A tank to their front was hit by a mine and its driver's legs shattered. A little while later the tank crew passed Dearden bearing their injured driver in a blanket, dripping blood. "Goodbye Canada!" they said. "We've done our bit!" and headed for the bridgehead, leaving him to ponder on the ominous significance of that *"Goodbye Canada."*

Now they were all across – Canadians, Jocks and Commandos. Next it was the Americans' turn. During the hour-long preparation for the assault, the Ninth Army artillery had fired no less than 65,261 rounds and a total of 1,500 heavy bombers had attacked a dozen airfields, supporting the defenders. Now the three regiments of General Hobbs' 30th Division started to cross at the villages of Buedrich, Wallach and Rheinberg. Almost immediately light German mortar fire started to descend upon their jumping-off places.

But nothing could stop "Roosevelt's Butchers", as the Germans were said to call the veterans of the 30th. Their storm boats headed straight along the lines of white tracer guiding them across the Rhine. The "Butchers" had fought and died at the Stand at Mortain; they had attacked at Aachen; they had beaten the élite of SS *Obersturmbannführer* Jochen Peiper's battlegroup of the "Adolf Hitler Bodyguard" in the Ardennes. Now they were going in for the kill.

Two of their storm boats were knocked out. One man was killed; another three were wounded. That was all. Minutes later the keels of their boats were across, grating on the mud and shingle of the east bank of the Rhine. Sporadic bursts of German fire erupted through the grey, swirling fog but mainly the enemy was mute. As Lieutenant Whitney O. Refvem, commander of the 117th Infantry's Company B, said afterwards: "There was no real fight to it. The artillery had done the job for us."

Within two hours the 30th Infantry Division was firmly established on the other side – at a cost of a couple of dozen of casualties. It was no different in the 79th Division's area southeast of Rheinberg. By dawn General Wyche had two regiments across and dug in. Prisoners told them "they had never encountered anything like it" (the artillery); "it completely stunned, scared and shook them."[8]

There was some hard fighting to come for the two American divisions before they could break out of the bridgehead. But for the time being they rested on their laurels, grateful that they had crossed one of the most imposing obstacles in the whole of Western Europe at the cost of a mere thirty-one casualties.

In the British sector, however, things were vastly different. All that long night the Commandos at Wesel had been engaged in the messy, costly business of house-to-house fighting in the smoking brick rubble of what was left of the Old Rhenish town.

It was fighting of the toughest kind, demanding strong nerves as men stalked and killed each other at ranges of less than twenty yards, every new corner heralding sudden violent death.

"One patrol [of Germans]," a sergeant of No 3 Troop, 1st Commando, reported later, "came down the railway line and we waited till we could literally see the whites of their eyes before killing them with Bren and Tommy guns. Later a section of Germans came across the field ... we just picked them off like sitting birds. They had no idea where the fire was coming from and simply lay flat on the ground ready to be shot."[9]

Occasionally, however, amidst this cruel house-to-house fighting in which no quarter was given or expected, there were moments of light relief. Dug in among some ruins, Corporal Cosgrave discovered to his astonishment that Hector was not what he was supposed to be; indeed he should have been named "Hectorine". For suddenly the supposed drake had laid an egg – and Corporal Cosgrave did not like duck eggs. So Hector was given away. But Cosgrave, one day to be a village bobby for thirty years, consoled himself with the knowledge they wouldn't starve now; they had just found a cellar filled with pig carcasses. There'd be "grub enough" while "this little lot lasted".[10]

Sometimes the humour of that long night was a little bitter too. A captured German colonel was brought down to the candle-lit cellar in which Mills-Roberts had set up his headquarters. The German was questioned and then was dismissed. As he left he turned to one of his captors and said loftily: "Do you mind carrying my bag for me?"

Mills-Roberts glared at him. "As a member of the master race," he retorted, "you can surely deal with something as small as that."[11]

Suitably abashed, the Colonel allowed himself to be taken away.

It was from this same cellar that Mills-Roberts decided to attempt to put an end to the fighting. His scouts had discovered that the HQ of the German Kampfkommandant Wesel, aptly named Generalmajor Deutsch, was located a mere hundred yards from his own. He decided to send a patrol under RSM Woodcock out to find him and order him to surrender.

The patrol came within yards of Deutsch's HQ. In German, someone shouted Mills-Roberts' request.

Deutsch shouted back his defiance. For a moment there was silence, broken only by the distant rattle of small arms fire elsewhere in the ruined city. Then suddenly Deutsch burst out of his cellar, machine pistol at his hip.

The Commandos didn't hesitate. Deutsch went down in a burst of Bren-gun fire to crumple on the rubble – dead. He was the first of four generals who would die on the Rhine before this terrible last week of March 1945 was over.

Just as the dawn fog started to disperse, curling itself like a grey cat round the dripping bushes and the great steaming shell holes that now pocked the fields on the other side of the Rhine, General Rennie, commander of the 51st Highland Division, decided to cross to find out what was holding up his stalled battalions around Rees.

There, and in Rees itself, where it would take his 1st Battalion the Gordon Highlanders forty-eight hours to clear the town, the situation was decidedly sticky; and Rennie the veteran wanted to know why. Throwing aside the apprehension that had gripped him ever since he had been ordered into the Rhine operation, he decided to confer with Brigadier James Oliver of his leading brigade.

They arranged to meet at a crossroads where, after some discussion, the familiar figure of the General in his duffle coat and balmoral bearing the red hackle of the Black Watch, set off in his jeep again for the rear. He didn't get far. Suddenly there was the thud and the obscene howl of a mortar bomb. Men of his old enemy the 15th Panzer Grenadier Division had spotted the lone jeep. It was a direct hit. The jeep careered to a halt, its back axle collapsing, smoke pouring from its ruptured motor. Horrified, the General's ADC rushed to the still figure sprawled out in the wreckage at an impossible angle. He shook Rennie and asked him stupidly if he were all right. But the General gave no reply.

Minutes later the nearest aid post confirmed the worst: Thomas Rennie was dead.

"Aye, he was a guid General," one of his beloved Jocks said later. "He wasna' a shoutin' kinda man." But for the time being the Jocks were not going to be told of the death of their general. Horrocks, who knew that the dead commander had "hated everything about it" (the Rhine crossing) though he did not know why, hurriedly crossed the damned river himself. All three brigades of the 51st were engaged in heavy fighting and "something had to be done quickly". He conferred with the three brigadiers and it was decided to give command temporarily to James Oliver while a successor was found. But it was also ordered that the rank-and-file should learn nothing of the death of their General.

"Like Wolfe and Nelson," as the regimental history of the Black Watch puts it, "he had been killed in the moment of triumph."[12] For now the Jocks he had loved so much were going in for the kill. And behind them would come those other Jocks of the Canada's "Hell's Last Issue".

Relaxing that morning after their successful crossing, watching the prisoners roll in, most of whom seemed "bomb-happy", Private Buchanan spotted his CO Major King approaching "with a roll of maps under one arm and a Tommy gun under the other". As he came closer they could all see the big smile on the officer's broad face. One of the infantrymen grinned and commented wryly, "If Major King looks that happy they must have dug up something real nasty for us to do!"[13]

They had. The "Hell's Last Issue" were to attack the village of Speldrop and relieve the two companies of the late General's Black Watch.

FOUR

Dawn came for the American combat crews at five thirty-eight British Double Summer Time on March 24th. The orderlies ran from hut to hut in those dozen or so camps scattered across France south of Paris, waking the glider pilots – both "virgins" and veterans – in readiness for the great drop. Being Americans they ate a huge pre-combat breakfast of steak, ice-cream and apple pie, washed down with gallons of coffee – "java" as they called it.

Reveille came for the British on the other side of the Channel at two forty-five. In blacked-out Nissen huts they breakfasted off dried egg and a sausage, plus as much tea as they could drink. If they were lucky and were "well-in" with the cooks it was "sarnt-major's tea", a thick pungent brew made in the tea bucket with tinned milk so strong that a spoon would stand upright in it. *If* they were lucky.

But in both the British and American messes of the 6th Airborne and the US 17th Airborne Division, they made the same standard joke: *"The condemned man ate a hearty breakfast!"* And it would be true. For nearly two thousand of those bold young Americans and Britons that March day, it would indeed be the last breakfast they ever ate.

The British took off first: the paras of the 3rd and 5th Brigades being carried by planes of the US Army Air Corps; the 6th Airlanding Brigade having their gliders towed by the RAF. By seven that morning they were collecting over Hawkinge, Kent, in streams that stretched as far as the eye could see, watched by gaping crowds below: 429 planes and gliders carrying 4,876 men.

Two hours later the Americans were airborne too, with the last of the gliders – 906 of them, towed by 610 transports – rising just after nine. One glider bore the legend:

"IF YOU CAN READ THIS . . . IT WAS HELL OF A LANDING!"

Like everything else in Montgomery's grandiose plan for conquering the Rhine, this airborne drop was going to be on a tremendous scale – even bigger than the drop on D-Day itself – with over
25,000 men, British, Canadian and American, being delivered on the
first morning. But unlike at Arnhem, the paras would drop *after* the
ground troops had commenced their assault. Montgomery did not
want to repeat the Arnhem fiasco which failed because Horrocks'
ground troops could not link up with the men of the 1st Airborne
before they were overwhelmed by the SS.

In essence, the plan envisaged the paras landing on the high ground
beyond the Rhine: the British and Canadians of the 6th Airborne,
veterans of Normandy, dropping to the north of Wesel; the
Americans – as yet untried, save from some ground combat during the
Battle of the Bulge – to the south. They would seize that high ground
and thus facilitate a quick breakout from the Rhine bridgehead. But
one thing had been overlooked by the planners. For this was the start
of "Flak Alley", as the long-suffering pilots of the RAF called it,
where the deadly 88 mm and 20 mm flak runs were located in defence
of the Ruhr factories, and the sixteen-year-old gunners and female
auxiliaries of the Luftwaffe had already been alerted. The paras were
flying into what was potentially a worse tragedy than Arnhem itself.

By eight o'clock the two streams, British and American, had rendez-
voused just south of Brussels to become the largest single-day
airborne operation of the war.[1] The entire sky train now took more
than three hours and twenty minutes to pass a given point and would
deliver over 17,000 paras and glider-borne infantry, plus their equipment, in a matter of two hours into the small area on the other side of
the Rhine. Nothing like this had been seen before; nothing of its kind
would ever be attempted again. It was unique.

As the British gliders flew over Waterloo, one officer-pilot turned to
his sergeant co-pilot, a soldier who had been retrained as a glider-
pilot after the heavy losses suffered by the Glider Pilot Regiment at
Arnhem, and said: "My great-great-grandfather fought at Waterloo." The unimpressed working-class non-com looked down at the
old battlefield below and grunted: "So did mine and it was probably your great-grandfather who my great-great-grandfather killed.
Try not to do the same to me today!"[2]

That perhaps apocryphal story was the sign of the times. Four years of "ABCA" and "Current Affairs" brainwashing by earnest left-wingers; Michael Foot's *Daily Mirror*, with its Jane strip cartoon and "soldiers' rights"; the *Picture Post* and its "new Britain", plus the Beveridge Plan and the rest of those great plans for a "Welfare State" had all had their effect. The "other ranks" had grown "bolshy". In three short months they would kick out the old man who had saved their hides back in 1940; who after years of struggle had taught them to fight and win; and who now waited for them down below. Just as it was for Montgomery, this was going to be Winston Churchill's last victory.

At ten o'clock that fine morning the top brass assembled on a rise about a mile from the shattered town of Xanten. They were all there: "Ike", "Monty", "Big Simp" and naturally that "former naval person" who wouldn't have missed this moment for the world. After dismissing his secretary, Jock Colville – now off on a personal adventure on the other side of the Rhine with a certain Captain Gill – Churchill had set out for the front at a quarter to nine that morning. En route he had suffered a series of minor mishaps: he had left his false teeth behind (they were later delivered to him by a dispatch rider carrying them in a handkerchief); he had had his cap knocked off by the gun of an armoured car; and he had had some difficulty in finding the VIP latrine. But now he was here and waiting, telling the assembled top brass: "I should have liked to have deployed my men in red-coats on the plain down there and ordered them to charge. But now my armies are too vast."[3]

Suddenly there was a "subdued but intense roar" as Churchill described it later, a "rumbling of swarms of aircraft". Churchill lurched to his feet and stumbled a few yards down the slope, yelling with delight: *"They're coming! ... They're coming!"*[4]

They were indeed. That great airborne force had reached the Rhine.

The slaughter started almost immediately. All along the high ground the waiting German gunners opened fire – and they could hardly miss as the great armada flew steadily onwards, gradually losing height, unable to change formation as the grey puffballs of flak exploded everywhere. "It was a heroic, a glorious and terrible sight," R. W. Thompson recorded as he watched the drop from a church tower. "I saw one Dakota in flames fail to land by inches. He was coming in perfectly when his wheels touched the telegraph wires and over he went in flames. An inch, a split second, and all would have been well. They had survived the worst. They were almost home." Choked with grief, the correspondent added: "The burning bodies of those young men are one of the images that can never be washed out. We did not speak for a long time and never of that."[5]

Alan Moorehead, the Australian correspondent, also reported the horror of that morning. "Indeed it was a wonderful sight. They passed only two or three hundred feet above our heads, the tow planes drawing sometimes one or sometimes two gliders and flying in tight formation. Then single planes with the parachutists waiting intensely inside for the moment to plunge out of the open hatches. Here and there among all these hundreds of planes one would be hit by ack-ack fire, and it was an agonizing thing to see it break formation and start questing vainly back and forth in search of any sort of landing field and then at last plunge headlong to the ground. Within a few minutes nothing would be left but the black pillar of petrol smoke and the unidentifiable scraps of wings, propellers and human beings."[6]

Yet another pilot and his crew had, as the American paras phrased it, "bought the farm".

For an eternity of three and a half hours, 1,572 planes towing 1,326 gliders, covered by 900 fighters, would continue the assault. Before it was over one hundred of the tows and gliders would have "bought the farm" and 332 would have been severely damaged.

Paras were dropping from the sky on all sides, their parachutes blossoming like a myriad tiny flowers against the sky, while the deadly four-barrelled 20 mm flak pumped shells at them and the low flying planes. Brigadier Poett, a veteran of airborne warfare, parachuted down into this maelstrom of flame and steel with his headquarters staff of the 5th British Parachute Brigade. "Within five minutes of jumping," he recalled later, "I had lost my Brigade Major, Signals Officer and Administrative Officer ... we had the hell of a lot of casualties."[7]

Even as the paras were struggling out of their harnesses, collecting themselves and moving out towards their objectives, the great Horsa and Hamilcar gliders began the long, slow, dangerous descent. It had been planned to release them at 2,500 feet but because of technical difficulties some of them were freed at 3,500 feet. The boys and girls manning the German flak did not need a second invitation. Grimly they set to work to slaughter the frail wood-and-canvas flying birds.

Laden with petrol, the gliders ignited instantly and plunged to the ground like flaming torches. One glider that was carrying a light Tetrach tank simply disintegrated in mid-air, sending its cargo of men hurtling to their deaths. Within the first few minutes, ten gliders were shot down and three hundred damaged.

Staff-Sergeant Victor Miller, a veteran of the terrible airborne fiasco on Sicily two years before, had almost given up hope of finding a landing site for his Horsa. Already he had seen a Halifax tow-plane go down in flames. Now his front was obscured by thick drifting smoke. "For God's sake," he shouted to his co-pilot, "if you see a space with gliders on it we'll have a go!" Suddenly, as if by a miracle, a hole opened in the smoke and he could see the farmland below. "I couldn't believe my eyes," he reported later. "I was looking at the very field we had been briefed to put our soldiers in!"[8]

But Miller's relief was short-lived. As he came lower he saw the field was full of German soldiers. He skimmed a road at tree-top height. One wing slammed against a pole and its tip snapped off. The Horsa shimmied crazily – then abruptly they were down, skimming across the ploughed field like a beetle across a pond. Almost immediately the Germans started pumping lead into the thin fuselage of the lame bird which had settled at last.

In those same few minutes, Sergeant-Pilot "Andy" Andrews almost "bought the farm" too. Flak had severely wounded his co-pilot and virtually shattered the controls. Somehow he brought the craft down and it slammed into the field in a huge cloud of mud and turf. At a tremendous speed the stricken glider careered forward. Sweating with fear and tension, Andrews somehow managed to miss a group of poplars. Then to his horror he realized he was heading straight at the wreck of another glider. "There was a bump on the left, then a lurch forwards followed by a crunching, splintering, break-up sound, as if every piece of plywood was disintegrating into matchwood."[9]

One of the casualties – thirty percent of the whole of 6th Airborne Division – that day was Canadian Broadcasting correspondent Stanley Maxted who had escaped from the catastrophe of Arnhem the previous September. His Hamilcar was hissing in to land among the terrible chaos of the landing zone when it took a burst of 20 mm shell fire. "There was an explosion that appeared to be in my head, the smell of burnt cordite. I went down on one knee. Something hot and sticky was dripping over my right eye and off my chin and all over my clothes."[10]

But again the Canadian survived, as he had at Arnhem. Minutes later he was being attended to at a British field dressing station.

One of the doctors at that station was Lieutenant-Colonel Watts. As he stared around that terrible slaughter ground of the gliders he thought dispassionately: "[It] looked rather like a fairground in the process of closing down ... only the still figures of the dead gave a grim reality to the scene. ... Everywhere gliders were burning or tilted at impossible angles, their noses wrecked and smashed into the churned-up earth." In one glider he noted the charred bodies inside, "the whole looking for all the world as if some monster had set a birdcage on a bonfire".[11]

Now the casualties were streaming in to the field dressing stations from all sides: men limping, men being carried by comrades, men being pushed in wheel-barrows like Guy Fawkes dummies on Bonfire Night.

Para-medic James Byrom, who had been through it all before in Normandy, found himself confronted with a severely wounded man he had known back in England, a tough little Geordie working-man whose motto had always been "Follow the crowd". "I've always followed the fucking crowd and I've always been reet!" he used to say. But now he had followed the crowd for the last time; there was no hope for him. Byrom remembered that another of the dying man's stock phrases had been "Whose side are ye on?", and this was the little Geordie's only articulate remark as he lay gasping on the blood-stained stretcher, listening to the medics' hollow reassurances that everything would be all right. "*Whose side are ye on?*" As Byrom wrote later: "He could already feel himself sinking into the anonymity of death and wished to be sure that we knew who he was."[12]

That terrible morning the 1st Canadian Parachute Battalion was taking casualties as bad as any of the hard-pressed 6th Airborne. It had landed in a forest and a large number of its men had been suspended by their chutes from the trees, hanging there helplessly, easy targets for the enemy snipers. One by one the Germans picked them off.

The Canadians' colonel, Lieutenant-Colonel Nicklin, had been trapped this way before, back in Normandy, but then he had managed to escape. Not this morning. As he dangled there, among the dead of his battalion like men suspended from gibbets, he too was picked off by a sniper and killed.

Among those trying to rescue the wounded and dying was Corporal Topham, the Canadian medic. He had seen two other medics shot down as they tried to reach one of the injured Canadian paras; now he decided to have a go. While he was tending the wounded man he was shot in the nose. Undaunted Topham carried him to safety. For the next two hours, in spite of the crude comments of his fellows about the state of his nose. Topham doggedly continued his work and even rescued three Canadians from a blazing carrier. For his efforts that day he would richly deserve the fourth Victoria Cross for bravery to be awarded to a Canadian soldier that month; he at least lived to receive his.

Jock Colville and his escort, the strange Captain Gill,[13] had just been talking to some of the airborne wounded when it happened. A shell landed close by and severed the arm of the airborne colonel's driver. Colville's air force tunic was drenched with blood.

Thus covered in gore and clutching some eggs given to him by some officers, Colville returned to his master on the other side of the Rhine, where he found him in the company of Montgomery and other top brass.

"They looked at my blood-stained tunic. What, they asked, had happened to me? I poured out what was, I thought, my exciting story," Colville wrote much later. Montgomery's reaction was completely unexpected. "Livid with rage" he rounded on the surprised Colville. How dare Colville, a civil servant, get in the way of the battle? He had deserted his post. "This is an intolerable act of insubordination!" he barked, eyes blazing with passion. "I shall ——"

"Before you say what you will do, Field-Marshal," Churchill interrupted the tirade, "pray remember Mr Colville is *my* secretary and not *yours*. It is for me and not for you to issue a reprimand."[14]

Later, when Churchill was alone with Colville, the Prime Minister told him: "I am jealous. You have succeeded where I failed. Tomorrow *nothing* shall stop me!" And then he added with a grin: "Sleep soundly. You might have slept more soundly still."[15]

Colville did not record his thoughts at that moment. The die had been cast. On the morrow Churchill would cross the Rhine, whether Montgomery approved or not.

As darkness began to settle over the dropping zones and some order was restored to the usual chaos of an airborne drop, the top brass of the XVIII Airborne Corps, under American General Ridgway, started to cross the Rhine in an Alligator manned by a British crew, who fired bursts of machine-gun fire into the smoke and gloom to their front every few yards. On reaching the opposite side, still clutching his World War One vintage rifle and with the grenades he wore as a publicity gimmick attached to his uniform, Ridgway dropped over the side and went up the bank. He came across a German soldier in a foxhole. The General halted abruptly and stared. The German stared back, just as intently. Suddenly Ridgway realized the German was dead. He breathed out hard and moved on.

The little party penetrated into a shell-shattered wood. An American para of the 17th Airborne raced up on a heavy farmhorse; he was wearing a top hat and his carbine was slung over his back like a cowboy's rifle. When he saw Ridgway he didn't know whether to dismount, present arms or take off his silk hat in welcome. But when he saw the Commanding General was smiling he simply smiled back.

Ridgway found the HQ of the 17th Airborne and, borrowing some jeeps there, moved off to "check with" the British. Suddenly he ran into a hectic little fire-fight. Loosing off a couple of quick shots, he dropped out of his stalled jeep just as a grenade exploded beneath it. Slightly wounded, he lay there in the darkness. In the echoing silence all around him in the brush he could hear men breathing hard. The question was: were they Americans or Krauts?

He saw some willows move slightly. Up came his rifle. "Put your hands up, you son-of-a-bitch!" he cried excitedly.

"Aw go and shit in yer hat!" a very American voice retorted.

On this confused night private soldiers, knowing that they might well die before morning, were not very impressed by general officers, even if they did get this far forward.

It was the same in the British lines as the fighting for the ridge line started to die down and the men prepared for the long tense night ahead. Colonel Ian Murray, commander of the Glider Pilots' Regiment, who had organized the evacuation from Arnhem in what seemed another age now, decided it would do the morale of his men good if he visited them and reassured them that everything was going well, in spite of their tremendous casualties (thirty-seven percent).

So as both sides began to dig in he went from pilot to pilot, whispering confidently: "You needn't worry. The Second Army is across the Rhine and we shall leave tomorrow."

This time he was right. The survivors would indeed leave on the morrow. But his men were older and wiser now, particularly after those eight long days in Holland. Out of the darkness Murray heard a cynical voice cry: "Yeah – that's what yer told us at Arnhem..."[16]

FIVE

Darkness was falling as the men of "Hell's Last Issue" reached the start line for the attack on Speldrop. It was going to be a tricky business, they knew. They were to advance behind a rolling barrage across an open field swept by enemy machine-gun fire and would have to cover eight hundred yards of open ground before they reached the little red-brick village, now shrouded in the fog of war.

Nervously they waited, smoking a last cigarette, taking sips from their water bottles, waiting for the guns on the other side of the Rhine to signal the start of the attack. With them were a few surviving officers of the Black Watch, who told the Canadians there were no more "Jocks" in Speldrop; they were "all dead or captured". And they warned the tense Canadian infantry to "shoot anything that moves because it'll be a Jerry. Don't take any chances. Too many men have died there already."[1]

Abruptly the 5.5s on the other side of the Rhine opened up. Great steaming holes, like the work of monstrous moles, appeared in the fields to the Canadians' front. This was it! Cigarettes were tossed away. Weapons were gripped in hands that were suddenly damp with sweat. Eyes took in the view with strange new clarity. In the carriers the drivers hit their buttons. The engines roared into life. Petrol stank on the night air. Suddenly all was noise and crazy activity.

"We crossed the open in staggered intervals," Corporal Sam Dearden recalled after the war. "I rolled out into the open knowing it would be rough even if the roads were free of mines. You could hear them shells crack as they passed over head."[2]

Next to Dearden in the wildly bucking Bren-carrier was a very

calm Lieutenant Isner, another Jock, though his family had origin-
ated not very far from this very place.

"I don't think they like us here," Isner commented mildly.

To their front a Typhoon came zooming in low, blue lights flickering the length of its stubby wings. Somewhere ahead in the bil-
lowing yellow smoke a German self-propelled gun scuttled for cover.
But the metal monster could not escape. Fiery-red rockets trailing a
fury of scarlet sparks hissed towards it. The self-propelled gun reeled
as if struck by a sudden tornado. It rattled to a stop, one track falling
behind it like a severed limb. Next moment it began to burn furiously.

Private Buchanan and his comrades of Major King's company
doubled to keep up with the British barrage which rolled inexorably
in front of the infantry, churning up the ground and showering the
soldiers with gouts of soil and pebbles, leaving huge brown smoking
holes everywhere.

"About two hundred yards from the town," Buchanan recalled
afterwards, "we began to pass the Black Watch dead. There was one
complete section of eight to ten men who had apparently been cut
down in a cross-fire."[3]

The Canadians had just skirted those stiff corpses, crumpled and
torn like rag dolls, when it happened. One hundred and fifty yards
short of Speldrop the British barrage *stopped.*

It was the "snafu" (situation normal, all fucked up) that Buchanan
and his battle-wise comrades had been expecting all along. They hit
the ground as one, knowing well what was soon to come.

With elemental savagery the German guns opened up on the pros-
trate Canadians. A few second later their thunder was joined by the
dreadful stomach-churning howl of the "moaning minnies", the
German multiple mortars. Rockets blazed into the sky, trailing black
smoke after them, then came plunging down on the helpless
Canadians. In an instant they were swamped by the enemy's counter-
fire.

Lieutenant Isner jumped to his feet. "Come on!" he yelled "If
we're going to be killed, I'd sooner get it from our guns than theirs!"[4]

Animated by the crazy logic of battle, carried away by a primeval
atavistic fury, the Canadians charged right into the renewed firing of
their own guns. Isner went down almost immediately. Buchanan was
bowled off his feet by an exploding shell. He lay there stunned for a
moment, gasping frantically for breath like a stranded fish. Somehow
he struggled to his feet, astonished to find himself unharmed. He

grabbed his Bren which had been knocked out of his hand by the explosion and doubled over to where Isner lay. As Buchanan recalled: "He hadn't been as lucky as I. He was finished."[5]

Now the survivors, gaps in their ranks everywhere, swept into the embattled village, firing as they ran. Buchanan let the first house have a quick burst of tracer. Like most German houses it had a cellar, with the cellar window just protruding above the ground: the ideal ready-made bunker. Buchanan dived forward after the burst and kicked open the door. Like a Western gun-slinger in a movie he fired from the hip, spraying the kitchen with .303. Suddenly his Bren died at his hip. He had emptied his magazine.

Frantically he fumbled to change it, heart thumping, brain racing electrically. Everywhere in the bullet-pocked kitchen lay dead Germans. They had been waiting for him all right. He crept into the kitchen, crunching over broken glass and china. He found the door to the cellar and opened it cautiously, a grenade in his hand ready to drop in at the first sign of enemy activity.

He was startled by a shout in broad Scots. "Don't shoot! ... For God's sake, don't shoot – *Black Watch here!*"

Hastily Buchanan stuck the cottar pin back in his grenade and yelled for the men to come up, one at a time. First up was a sergeant, "a brave man to stand on those steps in the face of Bren gunfire", as Buchanan admitted. The sergeant looked at the panting Canadian and said glumly: "You've shot three of my men."

Buchanan was horror-stricken. "My God, I'm sorry mate!" he gasped. "But your officers told us you lads were all dead or captured!"[6]

The sergeant shrugged; then he explained that the survivors of the trapped Black Watch companies had held off the German paras with their entrenching tools and bayonets when they had run out of ammunition. They had risked maiming or worse by picking up the German stick grenades flung into the cellars and tossing them back at the enemy. Then, in the tragic confusion of battle, some of those same Jocks who had held out for nearly forty-eight hours against all the enemy could throw at them had been killed in the moment of rescue – by their own side.

Corporal Dearden also ran into the survivors of the ill-fated Black Watch. "Don't stop here!" they yelled to the Canadians as they prepared to halt their carrier. "He shoots through these houses any time he feels like it! Leave your vehicle and join us in the trench!"

Dearden and the rest heeded the warning, but there was going to be no nice protection beneath six foot of earth for them. They had to keep attacking. They continued to advance against stiff machine-gun fire. But that was not the worst of it. There were German snipers everywhere, lurking in the ruined, smoking shells of houses or buried down deep in the piles of brick rubble.

Dearden himself was hit in the pocket by a sniper but luckily escaped injury. He and his comrades now started "mouse-holing" – burrowing their way from house to house without exposing themselves to the dangers of the street, where night had been turned into day in the lurid angry flames of the burning houses. But in the tight dark confines of the houses and tunnels, where officers were not fully in control, the Canadians lost touch with each other and the survivors of the Black Watch. Now "friend and foe killed not only each other but their friends too." As some of the tougher Canadians said with a cynical shrug: "It's just tough shit. Tell the padre…"

Buchanan's group were now engaged in a savage bout of house-to-house fighting in the burning village. As he recalled later: "Not many prisoners were taken … if they didn't surrender before we started on the house, they never had the opportunity afterwards."[7]

The men of "Hell's Last Issue" had been well trained in the highly lethal techniques of house clearing in combat, which demanded nerve, resolution and speed. They needed all these qualities and more. A grenade flung through a shattered window. A brave man dashing forward at full tilt to spray the interior with bullets from his Sten or Bren gun. A boot slamming down the door. Then bursting in, shooting any German who was still alive. It was no use surrendering now. The Canadians' blood was up, they weren't taking prisoners. And this from room to room, from house to house, with "tail-end Charlie" being posted at the stairs to the bombed cellar – just in case someone decided to make a last suicidal charge from that direction.

Invariably the Canadians took casualties. Buchanan saw one green replacement throw a grenade into a German-held house and run straight in after it, *before* it had exploded. "He was blown right back out. He had gotten excited and it had cost him his life."[8]

This terrible night the Canadians certainly needed good nerves and resolution.

Some time just before dawn on Palm Sunday, March 25th, another "Jock" with a German name, a certain Sergeant Riedel, took over

what was left of Buchanan's platoon. Gathering the survivors together in the ugly white light of the false dawn, he pointed to an
orchard from which heavy firing was coming. "Get that objective," he
told them, "and we have done the job."

The Canadians moved out in single file, crouching like Indians on
the warpath, approaching the unsuspecting Germans dug in in the
orchard from their blind side. Then Riedel shouted "Charge!" and
they were off: "Throwing 36s, firing all our weapons and doing a lot
of yelling, we were into them before they could turn round their MGs
on us. It was all over in a few minutes. They threw up their arms and
yelled '*Kamerad!*'"[9]

It was only later when the heat of battle had fled from their bodies
that the survivors realized what they had been up against – and the
realization made them shudder. They had been facing the "Green
Devils", the German paras, who had outnumbered them two to one.
Not only that, but in the German positions they discovered three
75 mm cannon with literally heaps of high explosive and armour-
piercing shells. As Buchanan put it: "No wonder the Black Watch had
been cut to pieces."

The men of "Hell's Last Issue" were not the only Canadians fighting
for their lives on that night of March 24th/25th. They had been
followed across the Rhine by the North Nova Scotians, who had
drawn a particularly unpleasant ticket in the crazy lottery of battle.
They were to attack those elements of the 15th Panzer Grenadier
Division dug in at a crossroads at the village of Bienen, not far from
where General Rennie had been killed.

The Maritimers had attacked at noon on the 24th. "My platoon
assaulted in a single extended wave," one of their officers recalled
after the war. "Ten tumbled down, nailed on the instant by fire from
two, maybe three machine guns ... The rest of us rolled or dropped
into a shallow ditch, hardly more than a trough six inches deep at the
bottom of the dyke. The Bren gunners put their weapons to their
shoulders but never got a shot away (I saw them after the battle, both
dead, one still holding the aiming position) ... A rifleman on my left
took aim at a German weapon pit and with a spasm collapsed in my
arms. His face turned almost instantly a faint green and bore a simple
smile."[10]

By nightfall the Maritimers had taken the northern part of the
village, but at a terrible cost: 43 men dead, 71 wounded. Casualties

had been nearly twenty per cent and still there'd be another day of very hard fighting before they finally captured the place.

The young officer quoted above went to report to his CO that night. But after seven months of almost constant combat he had reached the end of his resources. "I hadn't any idea apparently of how far gone I was emotionally. Instead of furnishing a coherent account I simply stood in front of him weeping inarticulately, unable to construct a sentence, even to force a single word out of my mouth."[11]

Two days later he was evacuated back to England. He was "out". But for the men of North Nova Scotia and those of the Canadian HLI who would soon have to come to their aid, there was still more hell to come...

Horrocks was pushing more and more troops and specialized weapons across the Rhine now, anxious to hasten the end of the fighting in and around Rees. He sent over the 454th Mountain Battery, armed with the 3.7 inch howitzers, familiar to the British public as a star turn in peacetime military tournaments as competing teams sweated and groaned to take their guns to pieces, cross obstacles and assemble them again at the fastest possible speed.

Now, however, in their first taste of real action, Captain McNair's gunners went through their paces in deadly seriousness. As one observer described McNair and his men: "For each situation in his street to street battle McNair had some suggestion for using his gun. He hauled it over rubble, rushed it round corners, layed it on a house that was giving trouble, dodged back again, prepared his charges and then back to fire again. He even took it to bits and mounted it in an upstairs room. 'Exactly which window is the sniper in?' he said and then when the sniper fired at him, 'Oh, that one' and layed his gun on it. ... The effect on the enemy was devastating."[12]

Within hours McNair and his gun had become the talk of the 51st Highland Division, famous for their part in the street battles of Rees.

But Horrocks also sent over some even more fearsome machines to finally break the stubborn enemy's will to fight – Crocodiles, the most awesome weapon of all.

Captain Wilson was commanding the troop of Crocodiles. They

reached the battalion they were going to work with just after dark on the night of the 24th. As the adjutant of the battalion came through the door Wilson resisted an impulse to cry out in astonishment. "The CO will see you in a minute," the officer said. Then he added: "Didn't we last meet in the middle of the Peloponnesian War?"

Wilson could hardly answer. The last time had seen the older man facing him now, he had been correcting his Greek Unseens at school; it was his former classics master! "Yes," he managed to croak. "About the sack of Melos."

That had been yesterday. Now on this Palm Sunday, Wilson led his troops of great lumbering Churchill tanks into the attack with the infantry. Together they crossed three hundred yards of open ground, dodging the AP[13] shells that came winging their way in white glowing fury; and then they were there, at the village. It was strangely silent, almost as if uninhabited.

Wilson gave his order, an order he had not given since before he had been wounded back in the autumn: "Prepare to flame!"

Slowly the long nozzle of the flame-thrower swung round towards the first building which looked like a barn.

"Flame gun – fire!" Wilson rapped.

A yellow rod of flame shot out of the cannon. It leapt roaring towards the barn. Now the Crocodiles began to "flame" the whole village, turning this way and that as the fearsome weapon aimed at one building after another, until the air stank of fuel and burning and the very paint on the turrets of their tanks started to bubble and pop like the symptoms of some loathsome skin disease. Then it was over. The few terrified survivors came staggering out of their hiding places, "wounded, blinded and burned, roughly bandaged beneath their charred uniforms". Wilson hardly dared look at them – his victims.

Later, when he returned to the infantry battalion's HQ, his former classics teacher had some letters waiting for him. One was from his mother. It said: "*We are proud of you.*"

While Wilson and his men massacred the unknown Germans in that Rhenish village, Winston Churchill and the brass were attending divine service in the open air. As Brooke noted in his diary: "The hymns were good and the parson, a Presbyterian, preached a good sermon."[14] But Churchill was intent on more than good hymns and good sermons; he was panting to get across the other side of the Rhine before events forced him to return to his duties in London.

A little later the British motored to meet Eisenhower, Bradley and Simpson at the corps headquarters of US General Anderson who commanded the corps to which the 30th and 79th American Divisions belonged.

Anderson explained the situation to his VIP visitors and then, after a light lunch al fresco, they all drove down the Wesel road to a colliery manager's house which stood on the bank of the Rhine and offered a wonderful view across the river to the ruins of Wesel and the US Army's treadway bridge.[15]

At this stage Eisenhower left to confer with Bradley. Unknown to Churchill, he was about to change the whole course of the war in Europe. He would send a message to Marshall, his chief in Washington, which was deliberately low-key and vague. It read: "The dash and daring in First and Third Army sectors have gotten us two bridgeheads very cheaply which can be consolidated and expanded rapidly to support a major thrust."[16]

As Bradley wrote later: "In my eyes it was an immense concession. It opened the way for me to draw a wholly new plan for the final conquest of Germany in which American commanders and forces would play the leading roles. I was immensely pleased. The prolonged British domination of our continental strategy was coming to an end; henceforth, Monty's role would sharply decline."[17]

As yet, however, Churchill did not know that his own conception of victory in Europe, with its effect on his post-war plans, was no longer valid. It would take him three more days to find out that his strategy was in ruins. Now he was intent on enjoying himself. As soon as Eisenhower had gone he turned to Montgomery and said happily: "Now *I'm* in command. Let's go over."[18]

"Why not?" Montgomery answered, to Churchill's surprise.

Simpson, returning from having escorted Eisenhower to his plane, was astonished to find Churchill and several other officers climbing into an American Navy craft for the trip across the Rhine. "Now that General Eisenhower is gone," Churchill called out with a boyish grin, "I'm going across!"[19]

They landed on the other side in brilliant sunshine and Churchill, puffing his big cigar, set off briskly to the sound of the battle.

Simpson said to Montgomery urgently: "This is no place for the PM. I'd hate to have anything happen to him in my army area!"

Then the American commander quickened his pace to catch up with Churchill. "If we keep going," he told the Prime Minister jokingly, "we'll soon be in the front line."[20]

Churchill relented, and they returned to their launch; but on their way back Montgomery suddenly seemed to be infected by Churchill's spirit of adventure. Later Churchill wrote wrily: "My adventurous host ... seemed ... to have one standard for Jock Colville and another for himself."[21]

"Can't we go down the river towards Wesel," Montgomery asked the US skipper, "where there is something going on?"

This was impossible, he was told, because of a chain stretched across the river to prevent the Germans from floating mines down it to destroy the Allied pontoon bridges. So Montgomery leaned over to Churchill, as one conspirator to another, and said: "Let's go down to the railway bridge at Wesel..."[22]

So they did. And even as Churchill scrambled nimbly onto one of the girders of the wrecked bridge, the shells were falling closer and closer, sending up huge jets of water. It was almost as if the German artillery knew that Churchill was there in person. Finally, one salvo actually hit the opposite end of the bridge.

An American officer drew up to Simpson. "Sir," he said, "we're bracketed already. One or two more tries and they may hit you!"

Simpson agreed. So, fearful that he would be blamed for the death of Britain's leading politician, he made his decision. "Prime Minister," he said very formally, "there are snipers in front of you. They are shelling both sides of the bridge and now they have started shelling the road behind you. I cannot accept the responsibility for your being here and must ask you to come away."[23]

Churchill hugged the girder and the look on his moonlike face reminded Brooke of a small boy on the beach being dragged away from his sandcastle. For a moment the assembled company thought Simpson would have to pry him loose. But then to everyone's relief he gave in and allowed himself to be taken back.

Later that day Brooke remembered something Churchill had once said: "The way to die is to pass out fighting when your blood is up and you feel nothing." Now he wrote to his wife: "He [Churchill] was determined to take every risk he could possibly take and if possible endanger his life to the maximum. I rather feel that he considers that a sudden and soldierly death at the front would be a suitable ending to his famous life and would free him from the never-ending worries which loom ahead."[24]

Two days ago Goebbels had noted in his diary: "The British Empire is creaking at every joint and sooner or later will be in the severest straits." That Sunday he heard about reports in the British press that Churchill had visited the Rhine, and he opened his diary again. "The old criminal," Goebbels wrote, "gazed at the destruction in the Wesel area through field glasses. Probably he will pride himself a great deal on that. One day he will go down in history as the destroyer of the European continent."[25]

But the "poison dwarf" had got the wrong man. It was not the rotund old man with the face of a benevolent Buddha who would help to destroy the future of Central Europe. That man was already back at his headquarters in Rheims, working out his new plan of strategy.

SIX

Still the fighting went on. The Canadian paras were now moving out of the woods where their colonel had been shot, and they were in no mood to play around with any Germans they came across that day.

Private Collins, who had never been in action before, remembers how his section flushed out one of the detested German snipers. "He came running out with his hands locked over his helmet. Fortunately, or maybe purposely, he had missed us. But one of the boys lifted him with a butt stroke of his Sten. He was hit so hard we just left him there and moved on."[1]

A little later Collins was present when some of his comrades brought in a shot-down Luftwaffe pilot. In spite of the fact that he was surrounded by tough-looking paras, the German was cocky, very cocky still; so much so that he was challenged to a fist-fight by a Canadian sergeant. Thus in the middle of a major battle the Canadian and the German fought it out with their clenched fists! According to Collins the German "gave an excellent account of himself but the sergeant knocked him down at last and he didn't wish to continue".[2] One isn't surprised.

A little later a German general tried to hold the paras back single-handed, firing at them with his machine pistol. The paras called upon him to surrender. He refused. So in the end a lone sergeant went out to stalk him. At ten yards' range he shot the general down and carved another notch on the butt of his rifle.[3]

Some Germans tried to surrender but were not given the chance. Under the command of Major Huw Weldon, one day to be a BBC television "personality", C Company of the 1st Ulster Rifles of the 6th Airborne were moving up through dead Americans of the 17th

Airborne when they spotted the Germans. "I saw a figure in a long German greatcoat rise to his feet," Staff-Sergeant Cramer recalled afterwards, "from the centre of a field and walk towards us with his hands up. The man was *Volkssturm* [German Home Guard], about fifty or sixty years of age, a long thin chap. Before we could do anything, three Americans let fly with their carbines and the figure fell. God we were angry! So was Major Weldon."[4]

Later, however, they succeeded in taking the rest of the Germans alive. The prisoners weren't very impressive. They flung themselves at their captors' feet and begged for mercy on their knees. It wasn't at all what Cramer had been expecting; these craven souls hardly bore any resemblance to the kind of German soldier he remembered from the training posters back home. Indeed, when Cramer handed them in at the battalion POW cage, the glider-pilot in charge snorted contemptuously: "Christ – can't you do better than this!"

But, pathetic as it seemed, the opposition could still cause plenty of casualties from their dug-in positions. When the Ulstermen started to count heads that day they discovered they had lost 16 officers and 243 other ranks, nearly a third of the battalion ...

"The Red Devons", as the men of the Devonshire Regiment called themselves, had also suffered heavy casualties in the last two and a half days. Corporal Dudley Anderson's platoon was now down to two-thirds of its original strength, and the rest of the battalion had experienced even worse casualties, with the killed, wounded and missing accounting for sixty-seven per cent of its strength. Now, however, Anderson's platoon and another units, sixty men in all, were going to have to assault twice that number of Germans dug in on a ridge.

They set out at dawn under the command of a Lieutenant Weeks. Six hundred yards from their objective the Germans opened fire. The "Red Devons" dropped as one into a ditch. "Don't get up in the same place you went down!" Weeks warned them. Then they were off again, zig-zagging crazily over the damp glistening fields. Men started to go down everywhere. But they were gaining ground; they were only four hundred yards away from the Germans now ...

"Come on boys, keep up!" Weeks cried. "Only one more ditch!"

Two hundred yards. They dropped again. One of Anderson's pals, Jack Nichols, was hit in the arm. Anderson, who had already taken part in two bayonet charges at the ripe old age of nineteen, thought it would be better to swop his Sten for Nichols' bayonet and rifle.

"There was no command. Someone started to climb out of the ditch and the rest rose with him. I found myself running with the others towards the German trenches. I could see the Germans plainly now, still firing their rifles. Our tank had stopped firing for fear of hitting us. There was no time to swerve or dodge, just run ... run as fast as your legs could carry you ... and don't forget to yell and scream at the top of your voice ... Never mind if some of your mates were falling or dropping behind. It was now just you or Jerry.

"The German trenches were only twenty yards away ... ten yards ... five ... I had picked out my German. Suddenly it was all over. The Germans were throwing down their arms and raising their hands. They had to be quick; some who were too late got shot. Not one of us had to use the bayonet but no one, least of all the Germans, had any doubts about our intention of doing so."[5]

They had done it. But behind them, lying very still in dew-damp fields, big ammunition boots sticking up to mark their position, lay those who had paid the butcher's bill: dead before they had really begun to live – dead before they even learnt the name of this place.

The survivors of the "Hell's Last Issue" were roused from an exhausted sleep just before midnight on that Sunday. They were to take part in yet another rescue operation: this time it was to help their comrades of the North Nova Scotias and the Argyll and Sutherland Highlanders, bogged down in heavy fighting at Bienen five miles away.

"As we moved into the streets of the town," Corporal Dearden recalled, "bitter fighting was raging in every street. Progress was slow. You tried to know friend and foe by the sound of his weapons. German machine guns fired faster than our standard Bren." He and the rest advanced deeper into the embattled village with their carriers. "Suddenly all hell broke loose. Fire tracer and everything criss-crossed the streets. I backed up the carrier a few feet and into a deserted building on the corner with a Bren gun which I set up to cover the streets."[6]

It was not till dawn that Dearden discovered to his dismay that he had set up his position on the grotesquely squashed bodies of two very dead German soldiers.

Buchanan, running full tilt in the confused fighting, had bumped into something in the glowing darkness which stopped him dead. To his horror he discovered that he was draped over the long barrel of an

88 mm cannon – and that cannon belonged to a monstrous 60-ton Tiger tank!

"All I could do was drop to the ground and yell to the others to get back. There was no movement from within the tank and I could see the hatches were open. The tank was bogged down almost to its turret in a manure pile with its barrel three feet off the ground."[7]

Buchanan lay there wondering what he should do. Had it been abandoned, this huge tank lying there on the top of the "honey-dew pile"? Or were the crew still hiding inside the steel shell, waiting for some unsuspecting Canuck like himself to come investigating? He decided to play safe just in case there was anyone lying "doggo". He slammed a 36 grenade inside and ducked as it erupted with a furious roar. Nothing stirred, but Buchanan was too scared to investigate any further. He left the Tiger "smoking".

"Progress was very slow," the war diary of the HLI recorded, "as the enemy fought like madmen. Isolated houses had to be cleared and proved most difficult. The enemy artillery and mortars poured shells into our troops continually. Again single paratroopers made suicidal charges at our advancing troops. They were consistently chopped down, but sometimes not before they had inflicted casualties on our sections."[8]

Private Buchanan and his comrades, sheltering in the basement of a ruined house, found themselves the sudden recipients of just such a German artillery bombardment and immediately began to take casualties – or so they thought. "A shell came through the window and exploded in the back room. When the smoke had cleared we counted noses. One man thought he was blind but his eyes were only filled with plaster and dust. Another had the funny bone on his elbow chipped off."[9]

However, the shocked Canadians were convinced they had one really serious casualty when they found "one of the men laying under a pile of shelves bleeding from the nose and ears. The stretcher bearer said he was dead and to lay him outside against the back wall." Dutifully they did so. But they were in for a shock. A little while later they were astonished to see "by the light of a smoky old lantern ... the man we had left for dead outside. He had been knocked unconcious and the rain had revived him."

But as the mist started to clear on the morning of March 26th, the fighting began to die down; the Canadians had almost worn the Germans down at last. They encountered a German 88 mm cannon dug in at the edge of the shattered village but hadn't the strength to tackle it themselves. Instead they whistled up a Priest self-propelled gun. The clumsy-looked SP fired two shells at the 88 mm and its ammunition exploded, with shells zig-zagging crazily in all directions into the dawn sky. And that was that. The shooting stopped.

While jeeps raced up to collect the wounded, the survivors, who had hardly any sleep for three long days began to sort themselves out. Looking round Private Buchanan thought, "We sure look like our regimental nickname suggests – Hell's Last Issue."

He was shocked, too, by the number of men missing from his own B Company. Mostly they were the young replacements and he told himself grimly: "The old saying of surviving a week at the front and your chance of living went up seemed to hold true."

Finally the survivors paraded and the Company Sergeant Major reported to Major King who had taken them into the attack: "Fifty-four men on parade – all the rest accounted for, sir."

They had lost half a company in those three days on the Rhine – but like Buchanan they were all proud of the fact that "they had never had a man taken prisoner, no man posted missing, and no ground once taken ever lost".

The next day they were issued with fresh grenades and ammunition, the gaps in their ranks were filled with replacements, and they were off again. There were new battles for "Hell's Last Issue" to fight.

Now the *Schlachtenbummler* ("battle tourists") as the Germans called them began to cross the conquered river to view the scene of death and destruction. Some, like war correspondent R. W. Thompson, were still shocked, their minds full of the terrible events of these last few days. "I remember the screeching of panic-stricken beasts beneath the harsh wheezing stutter of the machine guns and the bursting squawk of the Bofors and the thunder and cracks of every kind of artillery ... The wet smack of spandau bullets on the earth wall on which we lay and the whang of bullets hitting the telegraph wires ... And I shall never forget the tragic sight of Dakotas in flames and the price paid in human life for victory. And overhead, above the flaming wreckage of aircraft and men, a lark trilled its spring song."[10]

Alan Moorehead was more interested in the German civilians he encountered in the "strange numbness, a kind of vacuum" behind the fighting troops. "Odd incongruities spring up in this unusual atmosphere. The bargee's wife continues to hang out the washing ... she clings to this routine as one sane thing in a world gone mad. The house beyond has collapsed like a house of cards ... but a man still digs a vegetable patch in the garden."[11]

Moorehead later saw a withered old man pasting up notices at the command of some enterprising Military Government official. They dealt with Allied financial reforms. "But it doesn't matter much; as yet there is no one to read them and since last night money ceased to count for anything anymore." Indeed, Moorehead noted that the old man had difficulty in finding enough standing walls on which to post his proclamations.

Others of these *Schlachtenbummler* encountered yet fresh horror and tragedy, even though the fighting was over. Gerard Mansell, at twenty-four years old the senior intelligence officer with 9th Corps, now pushing out from the bridgehead, strolled through the ruins which he later described as "apocalyptic". "Destroyed towns, deserted countryside, hostility in the air. Dejected prisoners – often old men or boys – drifting back past us in crowds, with refugees and displaced persons. Chaos and a feeling of disintegration and putrescence everywhere."[12]

Mansell was used to such things, however. He had fought at El Alamein and had taken part in the assault landing in Sicily and Normandy. But as the long column of vehicles rolled through the shattered village of Weldar, Mansell did not yet know that his own younger brother had been murdered here the previous night.

Bob Mansell was one of the glider pilots who had brought in the 6th Airborne on March 24th. During the confused fighting he had fallen into German hands, but somehow he had escaped and for three days had been trying to make his way back to Allied lines. He had not succeeded. On the night before, he had been cornered by a band of fanatical Hitler Youth teenagers. They had slaughtered him savagely among the ruins through which an unsuspecting Major Mansell now drove.

But not all was gloom on the Rhine as March approached its end and fighting started to peter out. Having successfully captured a large sugar factory at the Rhenish city of Rheine, the victorious infantrymen discovered to their delight that the cellars were filled with Russian "slave workers". They weren't particularly pretty but they were female – and willing!

Unknown to the ecstatic infantrymen busily engaged "getting off their oats" (in the parlance of the time) with the Russian girls, German snipers had concealed themselves around the huge factory. Suddenly small arms fire broke out. It didn't last long but one jeering crowd of infantrymen saw their platoon sergeant borne out of the cellar by the stretcher-bearers, face down on the litter, his trousers round his ankles, a smear of red blood on his white buttocks.

"Shot on the job," he moaned. "Ain't there no justice? Shot on the job..."'

As his men jeered later, when they heard the sergeant had received a medal (for services in Holland), "When yer kids ask yer, Sarge, how yer won yer medal – yer'll never dare tell 'em!"

Private Bedford of the 53rd Division's Manchester Regiment was also involved in medals that same day. Ever since Normandy his company commander had regularly been putting his men's names into a hat, the ones drawn out first to receive whatever medals were going. Now just before the Manchesters crossed the river – much annoyed because Churchill had done it before them – Bedford's eccentric company commander decided to hold another of his "raffles", as the men called them scornfully. Once again, to Bedford's disgust, he failed to pick himself out a "MM" or even a "mentioned in dispatches".

Now, however, as they crossed the Rhine and started heading through the first German villages, the Manchesters were surprised to find the Germans greeting them as if they were liberators rather than conquerors. "Back in Normandy," Bedford recalled forty years later, "the French hadn't liked us one bit. They had actually shot at us and it was rumoured in the Division that we'd shot at least twenty French civilian snipers, including women. Now here we were in Germany – and the Jerries were actually waving at us!"[13]

The surviving British glider pilots had also received a strange reception on arrival back at Down Ampney airfield, to which they had been flown on the 25th, leaving the 6th to fight without them. There they were met by an over-zealous Customs official, demanding that the battle-weary pilots should fill out entry-to-Britain forms. "He actually wanted to know if we had anything declare," Sergeant Andrews recalled indignantly. But the Customs man was soon told "to buzz off" according to Andrews, "or words to that effect".

Another group of glider pilots, Americans this time, decided to relax in Paris after the trials and tribulations of the Rhine drop. A certain Flight Officer John Lowden of the 440th Troop Carrier Group was given the task of finding suitable accommodation. He worked his way down the list of hopelessly overcrowded Parisian hotels until finally he found an empty place. It turned out to be a brothel.

The first bunch of officers set off for the weekend and came back on the following Monday demanding to speak to "that sonovabitch Lowden". Apparently, although they had had a "great weekend", they had all had their money stolen. Lowden himself went to Paris to "investigate", accompanied by one of his friends. The matter was soon cleared up, however, and the madam generously offered the two glider pilots a free room for the night. They accepted gratefully and asked for twin beds.

"Twin beds!" she exclaimed. "In *my* place? Surely, sir, you jest."

But the two pilots insisted; they were dog-tired. They just wanted to sleep. However, no twin beds could be found and in the end they compromised. They curled up together in one of the whores' double-beds.

A couple of hours later the two of them were startled out of their exhausted sleep by a thunderous knocking on the door. Lowden, in his underwear, opened it to be confronted by two of the biggest American MPs he had ever seen. As he let them in, "their eyes really lit up", and he knew why. "They had found two officers in bed together – *in a French whorehouse!*"

As they went out Lowden heard one of them say to the other: "Jesus, these Air Force types think of *everything!* Maybe they really are winnng the war . . ."[14]

On Tuesday, March 27th, Montgomery decided the Battle of the Rhine was won. His three armoured divisions – the 7th, 11th and the Guards Armoured – were poised to make their breakout. Now he sat down at his headquarters in Venlo to draft the signal he would send to Eisenhower about the future strategy for his Twenty-first Army Group.

Two days before, when he had last met Eisenhower on the Rhine with Churchill, he had demonstrated how he would break out of the bridgehead using Simpson's Ninth Army, heading north until he reached the Elbe; there one wing of his armies would head straight for Berlin. After all, as Eisenhower himself had once told him back in '44, Berlin was "the main prize".

Eisenhower had listened and then made his own exposition to

Churchill and the rest of the top brass. He made no mention of any great changes of plans. Nor did he refer to any decision to remove Simpson's Ninth Army from Montgomery's command. More importantly, he accepted Berlin as the ultimate objective without comment.

So, flushed with his victory on the Rhine, Montgomery now set about drafting what he in his innocence no doubt thought was merely a formal outline of his plans for capturing that "glittering prize".

Every war produces its own heroes. But it had taken three years of defeat after defeat for Great Britain before World War Two produced its first hero: Bernard Law Montgomery, who thereafter would place his own particular imprint on Britain's conduct of the war.

The son of a bishop, who neither drank nor smoked (he was, however, an occasional gambler), whose wife had died years before, he was a different kind of general from the kind the British were accustomed to. He cared little about his dress – the King himself had once reprimanded him on that score – affecting shabby civilian clothes and more than once he had made public appearances carrying a ragged old green "gamp". He was small, too, hollow-cheeked and undersized, totally unlike the red-faced, tall, heavy generals – "the hearties" of his generation.

He talked to his men. Unlike his contemporaries who left "that sort of thing" to their NCOs, he seemed to want to let his soldiers know why they were fighting or for what. It might have been one of his many publicity gimmicks, like the berets, the badges and the free cigarettes; but it worked.

Yet in spite of his democratic approach there was still plenty of upper-class Britisher about "Monty". He was aloof, not given to tolerating fools gladly, and still a product of Britain's imperial past. Foreigners might be quaint, even interesting; but they were not British and therefore they couldn't possibly know as much as a Briton. This attitude, plus his egocentric, ascetic teetotalism, certainly did not endear him to the rugged "hail-fellow-well-met" type of American general.

Patton called him "a silly old fart" (although Patton was two years older than he was).[15] Bradley said: "Montgomery is a third-rate general and he never did anything or won a battle that any other general could not have won as well or better."[16] Even Eisenhower, who had tolerated Montgomery's "holier-than-thou" attitude longer than most, told writer Cornelius Ryan long after the war: "He

[Monty] got so damned personal to make sure that the Americans and me in particular had no credit, had nothing to do with the war, that I eventually stopped communicating with him ... I was just not interested in keeping up communication with a man that just can't tell the truth!"[17]

Montgomery, however, seemed quite oblivious of the Americans' hostility this cold Tuesday in March as he drafted his cable to the Supreme Commander: "Today I issued orders to Army Commanders for the operations to begin ... My intention is to drive hard for the line of the Elbe using the ninth and second armies. The right of the ninth army will be directed on Magdeburg and the left of the second army on Hamburg ...

"I have ordered ninth and second armies to move their armoured and mobile divisions forward at once to get through to the Elbe with all possible speed and drive.

"My TAC HQ moves to the northwest of Bonninghardt on Thursday 29th March. Thereafter my HQ will move to Wesel, Munster, Widenbruck [sic], Herford, Hanover – *thence by autobahn to Berlin I hope*" (author's italics).[18]

It was a pious hope ...

PART IV

Return to Arnhem

Six feet away from this huddled decayed ruin of a man ... is a great bloated thing so unhuman that it's hard to distinguish him from the earth ... He too was once a Canadian infantryman. Dust to dust they say ... if they had seen this ... It is not dust ... it is disease, the antithesis of dust. Dust is clean. This is foul. These are the glorious dead.
 Corporal Alexander McKee, Arnhem, May 1945

ONE

By the morning of Wednesday, March 28th, 1945, each of the four American armies in Europe – the Ninth, the First, the Third and the Seventh – had a firm bridgehead across the Rhine. Indeed, Patton had two: at Oppenheim and in the Rhine Gorge. But Patton wasn't satisfied. He wanted more. Carried away by his usual egomania, not only would he show he could beat that "silly old fart" Montgomery; but he would also outdo his fellow army commander, for whom he cherished no great respect. He decided to cross the Rhine once more. Again it would be a manoeuvre without any tactical or strategic purpose – but it was mighty good for Patton's inflated ego.

Before first light that morning, two regiments of the 80th US Infantry Division staged what the official history calls "a noisy little war" at Mainz on the Rhine and the River Main a few miles away. It was, indeed, all sound and little fury. Following a half-hour artillery preparation, men of the 80th's 317th Infantry slipped across in assault boats. The Germans on the other side opened up with 20 mm flak cannon. The surface of the great river glowed with reflected light as the hail of tracer shells hissed to meet the Americans. Surprisingly, not a single GI was injured, though many of them were scared enough.

Once they were across, the Germans threw in two small counter-attacks; but the GIs held them off easily. By the end of the day the Americans would have captured the city of Wiesbaden, opposite Mainz, and more than 900 Germans would have surrendered. So Patton had successfully crossed the Rhine for a second time and captured an important city on the *autobahn*, which ran south-east, without having lost a single soldier. It was to be the final American crossing – officially at least.

Some time later he would come to attend the inauguration of the Rhine Bridge built by the American engineers at that crossing site. Here a Major-General Ewart G. Plank, his host, would hand him a pair of outsized scissors to cut the ceremonial ribbon. True to his image and scowling with his "war face number one" (as he called the grimaces he practised in front of the mirror in the privacy of his bedroom) he would snort: "What are you taking me for – a tailor? ... *Goddammit, give me a bayonet!*"[1]

Hastily a bayonet was brought and Patton slashed through the silly ribbon with a single blow. Honour thus satisfied, Patton departed to continue his war in the heart of Bavaria, looking for the mythical National Redoubt which the Nazis had supposedly built there. Perhaps too he thought he could still find death in battle yet; for he always subscribed to the romantic notion that "The proper end for the professional soldier is a quick death inflicted by the *last* bullet of the *last* battle!"

But General Patton would not die in battle like so many of his soldiers. He would die in a hospital bed before the year was out, less than fifty miles from where his soldiers had captured another bridgehead this cold March day. "*General Patton Dies Quietly in Sleep*" the newspapers would headline the front page story. It was a funny kind of ending for "Old Blood an' Guts".

That same day, March 28th, the US Army newspaper, the *Stars and Stripes*, reported yet another "crossing" of the Rhine, made by a lone GI named Augustus Winkelknopfer of Crawling Valley, Wisconsin. Interviewed by the paper's reporter, Winkelknopfer was asked: "Is it true you were carried by a Rhine-Maiden?"

"Hell, yes," answered the Private First Class, munching a knockwurst sausage.

And how had Winkelknopfer found his Rhine-Maiden, the reporter asked.

"It was easy," Winkelknopfer told him. "We were bivouacked one night in a castle high up on a crag. It was a foggy night and I went down to the dungeon. I heard this fluttering of wings and there she was, drinking a flagon of Munich beer, flapping her wings and reading *Mein Kampf*."

Next morning, according to Winkelknopfer, after she had finished cleaning her teeth with beer, she agreed to take him across the Rhine. So, tied to her by a large rope, he took off. "Down below I see barges crossing the Rhine. Up in a cloud I see two other of these babes flying around with radios for Nazi reconnaissance, so I shoot them down. She keeps going,"

The reporter wondered whether Winkelknopfer's landing was hard.

"Nah, nothin' to it," he answered. "She leaves me down in a field, easy as a lark. I give her another drag of the brew which I keep, say 'Dankeschoen' and she takes off and and flies away howling *Gotterdammerung*."

Tongue in cheek, reporter Private Bob Wronker noted: "That is all there was to Winkelknopfer's crossing. On the way to rejoin his unit, a second lieutenant who witnessed the landing fined him for fraternizing with the enemy."

It wasn't a very good spoof, but it illustrated one significant point. The crossing of the great river, which had cost so much British and Canadian blood, had become little better than a joke.

On the same morning that Patton's 8oth Division successfully completed the last American crossing of the Rhine, General Eisenhower arrived promptly at his HQ in Rheims at his usual time of quarter to eight.

It was located just behind the shell-pocked railway station, down a narrow side-street, in the former French technical school, the College Moderne et Technique. Here on the second floor overlooking the street, packed with the usual MPs, both American and British, Eisenhower had his office. It was a sparsely furnished room, even spartan, with Eisenhower's desk placed on a raised platform where undoubtedly some obscure French technical teacher had once had his.

He said a crisp good morning to his Chief-of-Staff, "Beetle" Smith, and then got down to work on the blue leather folders bearing the highest security legend: "*For Eisenhower's Eyes Only*".

Ancient French locomotives in the shunting yard puffed and clattered back and forth, and the two-and-a-half ton trucks of the "Red Ball Express" rumbled through the narrow streets, but Eisenhower barely noticed the noise as he considered the two most important documents in that folder.

One was from General Marshall, the US Chief-of-Staff. Marshall queried, now that the German front seemed on the point of collapse, whether it might not be wise to advance on the Nuremberg–Linz or Karlsruhe–Munich axis to prevent any German resistance being formed in Bavarian–Austrian alps.

The other was from Field-Marshal Montgomery – those nine terse paragraphs that he had drafted the previous day. It made Eisenhower feel "like a horse with a burr under his saddle". For Montgomery wasn't asking; he was *demanding*.

In Montgomery's view, the Anglo-American armies lacked the supply and maintenance capacity for two major drives from the Rhine. In his opinion, there could be only one – and that, naturally, was his. It would need "all the maintenance resources … without qualification". And, Montgomery warned solemnly, "If we attempt a compromise solution and split our maintenance resources so neither thrust is full-blooded, we will prolong the war." Time was "of such vital importance", he added "that a decision is required *at once!*" (author's italics).[2]

For most of that long chill March day, Eisenhower sat at his desk, chain-smoking his Lucky Strikes and brooding about those two cables. By the end of the day he would have made his most important decision of the whole long bloody campaign…

Five years before, Eisenhower had returned from the Philippines as an obscure lieutenant-colonel. After thirty years of service, he could look forward to nothing more than an Army pension and retirement to one of those southern garrison towns where he could play a little golf in the sunshine and be close to the medical and PX facilities. Indeed, he was so obscure that when he was featured in a magazine after an Army exercise, his photo was captioned "Lt-Col. D. D. Ersenbeing".

Then things had started to move fast. He was promoted to general over the heads of hundreds of senior officers. Marshall took him up. He was ordered to Washington. Then in 1942 he was recommended for the command of all Allied forces in Europe. That June he told Mamie over the phone: "Looks like I'm going to London next week. I'm going to be in command there."

"In command of what?" Mamie had asked.

"*Of the whole shebang!*" Eisenhower had told her triumphantly.

And now here he was, Supreme Commander of the most awesome military machine the world had ever seen. Over the last thirty-six months his career had been like that of some twentieth-century Grant. Millions of men were under his command. Time and time again, in Africa and in Europe, he had been forced to take tough decisions, which had hardened and matured him, made him resistant to the carping criticism of the envious, the inferior, the politically and militarily impotent.

But his character had always been flawed by one fatal weakness: even when he had made a decision, he seemed incapable of sticking to it. Over and over again he had wavered, backed off, modified. Sitting there alone, smoking his "Luckies", Eisenhower realized he now faced another difficult decision this day, one that would bring down upon him a barrage of violent criticism, in particular from the British, if he did not meet Montgomery's demand.

Much had changed since he had first gone to London, an unknown major-general appalled by the terrible smell of boiled brussels sprouts that seemed to lie over everything. He was no longer awed by the British or frightened by Churchill. And no doubt he already realized that his military career was nearing its end and – again like General Grant – that he might soon be selected by one of the two political parties as a presidential candidate.

So he must have been thinking that day that America's interests came first, regardless of the political future of Central Europe. In essence, what did Berlin matter?

Bradley, he knew, would never accept any subordinate role in future operations. "Brad" had told him unequivocally: "You must know, Ike, I cannot serve under Montgomery ... for if Montgomery goes in over me I will have lost the confidence of my command."

He knew, too, that his senior commanders were all strongly anti-British now, totally opposed to letting the British take the kudos of the final victory. As they put it, it was a matter of the prestige of the US Army. Whether it was this that concerned them or the fact that they might lose the limelight to Montgomery, it was all the same to Eisenhower that day. Patton had once called him "the best God-damned general the British have got", but he could not afford to have the great American public believe that was true, especially if he were to enter politics after the war.

Besides, why should he pander to the British any longer? For every one division they fielded now that March, the American Army had three. Montgomery had proved himself ungrateful time and time again; and as for Churchill, he was always poking his fingers into military pies which did not concern him.

Undoubtedly, as he mulled over the problem of the future strategy for the last battle that day, Eisenhower must have wondered what the verdict of history would be if he gave the hated Montgomery his head.

What would history's judgement be on himself? Would he be risking his own political future?... By three that afternoon he had made up his mind. He started drafting three cables outlining his new strategy: one went to Marshall, the second went to Montgomery and the third – remarkably enough – went to "Uncle Joe". It was a sign of Eisenhower's status and mood this March that without recourse to Roosevelt and Churchill, not to mention the US Chiefs-of-Staff back in Washington, he was also communicating directly with no less a person that the Soviet dictator, Josef Stalin.

At five minutes past seven that evening his cable to Montgomery finally went out. "As soon as you have joined hands with Bradley [after the encirclement of the Ruhr] the Ninth US Army will revert to Bradley's command ... Bradley will be responsible for mopping up ... the Ruhr and with the minimum delay will deliver his main thrust on the axis Erfurt–Leipzig–Dresden to join hands with the Russians." And, after reading the draft, Eisenhower added one last line in pencil: "As you say, the situation looks good."[3]

It did – but not for Bernard Law Montgomery. For as a shocked Montgomery would soon read, Eisenhower had written: "You will see that in none of this do I mention Berlin. So far as I am concerned that place has become nothing but a geographical location." Worse still was the cable's last paragraph indicating Eisenhower's role for the victorious Twenty-first Army Group, now poised on the Rhine. Montgomery would "cross the Elbe without delay, drive to the Baltic coast at Lübeck and seal off the Danish Peninsula".

The British and Canadian Armies had been reduced to nothing more than flank cover for Bradley's armies. The American top brass had had their revenge on Montgomery at last.

TWO

Seventeen hours after Eisenhower sent that cable, the end of all Mont-gomery's hopes for a triumphal entry into Berlin, another obscure major-general of 1940 who had since risen to the highest office was also sending an urgent telegram to one of his field commanders.

Fretting at the glory being earned by the British, Americans and Canadians on the Rhine, Charles de Gaulle wired the commander of his First Army, General de Lattre, whose men had been on the Rhine since November 16th, 1944: "My dear General, you must cross the Rhine even if the Americans are not agreeable and even if you have to cross in rowing boats. It is a matter of the greatest national interest. Karlsruhe and Stuttgart await you – even if they do not want you."[1]

Sensitive as always about his own position and prestige – and *la gloire de la France* of course – de Gaulle wanted the world to see that he and France were playing a full part in these world-shaking events on his country's frontier. True, he had once stated that the Anglo-Americans should be allowed to do the fighting and be killed; France would need all the soldiers she could muster for the problems of the post-war period. But now he was prepared to sacrifice French lives for the sake of the world publicity he hoped to achieve by a French crossing of the Rhine – the great river that France had always claimed was not just a German waterway but her border with France.

De Lattre gave the task to portly, heavily-moustached General Monsabert, who was ordered to cross on the night of March 30th at the German town of Speyer. Two years before, the Corps Commander had been loyally supporting the regime of Marshal Pétain in North Africa; he had rallied to the Allied cause only when it seemed the Anglo-Americans would succeed in beating the Boche there. Like most of his fellow senior commanders he was not a dedicated Gaullist. But he was French and so, naturally, he understood the importance of a crossing for France.

There was one catch, however. Devers, commanding the US Army group to which de Lattre's First Army belonged, together with General Patch's Seventh Army, was reluctant to have the Frenchmen getting in the way, more especially as Stuttgart had been specifically declared part of the US Army's zone of operations. As a result, dependent as it was upon the Americans for supplies, the First Army had not been issued with the requisite bridging and boats for an assault crossing.

But Monsabert persisted, and soon he was told that a number of rubber dinghies were on their way to him. They had no outboard motors, no steering, and were not as sturdy as those used by the Americans. But they were boats and they could be paddled across.

But where were the boats?

All that day the men of the 3rd Regiment de Tirailleurs Algériens waited with growing impatience for the promised boats, knowing that the eyes of General de Gaulle himself were upon them, waiting for the historic crossing. In the end the promised craft arrived – one single rubber dinghy.

The reaction of the Colonial soldiers is not recorded. But honour had to be satisfied. So a certain Sergeant Bertout and ten of his men clambered into the boat and laboriously rowed themselves across the Rhine. It is doubtful whether the Germans realized in the darkness that they were being invaded by *Franzmänner* for the first time since the days of Napoleon. Or perhaps they did not take the "invasion" seriously. At all events they did not react till daybreak, when they started shelling a second crossing at the small town of Germersheim.

There the crossing turned into a tragedy, with only three boats reaching the other side of the Rhine; and the "bridgehead" of 50 metres by 150 metres was only held because the French artillery managed to pound the German positions all day long and prevent the Boche from counter-attacking.

Eventually the Americans took pity on the French. The neighbouring American Corps Commander, Major-General Edward A. Brooks, agreed to let twenty French vehicles cross the Rhine using the American bridge at Mannheim.

The wheel had nearly turned full circle. The scruffy bunch of one-time collaborators, renegades, ex-Maquis, *pied noirs* and North

African colonial soldiers had managed to do what Leclerc had failed to do back in November; they had crossed the Rhine. Aptly enough the date was April 1st, 1945 – April Fool's Day.[2]

With good-humoured cynicism they called themselves "the Nijmegen Home Guard"; for ever since their first disastrous attempt to cross the Rhine at Arnhem back in September 1944, they had been stationed in and around that Dutch city guarding what was known as the "Island".

Between the River Waal at Nijmegen and the Lower Rhine at Arnhem, both towns being in view of each other because they stand on high ground, there is a stretch of low-lying land of about eight miles in length, surrounded by rivers on three sides and a marsh to the west. The Romans called it the "Island of the Batavians", the latter being the original inhabitants of that country. Now the Island was guarded, as it had been all that bitter winter, by the men of the 49th Division.

The 49th had not had a particularly good war. A territorial division, recruited mainly in the north-east of England, it had spent two years in Iceland where it had adopted the polar bear as its divisional insignia. On returning to England for the Invasion, their new commanding general ordered the polar bear's head to be *raised*. It seemed to him that the bear's hanging head reflected the mood of his men who had taken on many of the characteristics of those dour Icelanders during their stay in that country.

In Normandy the 49th had experienced severe fighting and had suffered heavy casualties. One of its battalions had broken down under shell fire. After two weeks only twelve of its officers had been left; as a consequence, the men had gone to pieces and discipline had collapsed, with both officers and non-coms removing their badges of rank. A new CO was hastily moved up to replace the first one who had been killed in action. But after only four days in command he was forced to report: "I have twice had to stand at the end of the track and draw my revolver on retreating men ... Three days running a Major has been killed ... because I have ordered him to help me, in effect, stop them running during mortar concentrations."[3]

Montgomery had sacked the unfortunate second CO and disbanded what was left of his battalion. Thereafter he had seemed to lose interest in the 49th Division. Two months later, after aiding the

Canadian Army in the clearing of the Channel ports, the Division had landed on the Island in the wake of the Arnhem failure. And there they had remained, cut off from the main body of the British Army, being placed under the command of the Canadian II Corps which believed the Island made an ideal sally port from whence to launch an attack on the northern flank of the German armies west of the Rhine.

In November, one month after the 49th had arrived there, the Germans had flooded the low-lying land, then blown the dykes. The few remaining Dutch farmers now abandoned the Yorkshiremen to the rubble, wrecked vehicles and knee-deep mud, complaining, as that blunt Yorkshire proverb has it, "There's nowt for nowt – and damned little for a tanner!"[4]

All that winter and early spring, while great events were taking place elsewhere – events they could only read about in their newspapers – the "Nijmegen Home Guard" stuck it out in the freezing mud, fighting an isolated mini-war that no one ever heard about.

Some of them were lucky and managed "to get their feet under the table" as the Tommies phrased it. They found a nice comfortable billet with a Dutch family and occasionally even discovered some pro-British Dutch maiden prepared to let them have a "bit of the other". But mostly they found the few Dutch people remaining in the Island a sober-sided lot who were less well disposed to the Tommies than the popular press suggested. After all Holland had the highest percentage of collaborators of all; fifteen per cent of the population had joined the Dutch Nazi Party in 1940 and 50,000 Dutchmen had actually *volunteered* for the SS.

On the other side of the Rhine, the relatives of those civilians among whom they lived were starving, especially if they were residents of the big cities. In Rotterdam, for instance, there was a daily ration of 300 grams of potatoes, 200 grams of bread, 9 grams of fat, 28 grams of peas and 5 grams of cheese or meat per person per day – and this in one of Europe's most thriving agricultural countries.

"My days were spent for the most part queueing for whatever the ration cards promised us," Henri van der Zee, who was then ten, recalled much later. "It was so cold outside that I still remember the tears of pain and misery turning to icicles on my cheeks."[5] By the spring of 1945 Rotterdam's rations hit rock-bottom and the daily ration per citizen was reduced to 230 calories, a quarter of what concentration camp inmates were allowed by the Nazis!

But for the most part, life on the Island for the average member of the Nijmegen Home Guard was dreary, dull and freezingly cold, enlivened only by night patrols: both British and German.

Private Dunkley, a nineteen-year-old with the 7th Battalion the Duke of Wellington's Regiment of the 49th, recalled those patrols many years later. "I remember one in December 1944 when we saw the 'hump'. A crisp cold night with a brilliant moon. We had donned white camouflage with our rifles wrapped in old sheets and we went out along the main railway line between Nijmegen and Arnhem. It was easier to make progress there than on the frozen ground, by stepping from sleeper to sleeper as we went forward up the track. In some places the embankment was down, only the rails spanned the gap, and occasionally we had to go up on the embankment. We were doing this when the patrol leader held up his hand indicating 'Stop'. We waited. Then he whispered back: 'Somebody or something is lying in the middle of the track.'"

The patrol leader crawled forward and beckoned for the rest of the infantrymen to come out. There they crouched in the brilliant moonlight with the wind howling eerily across the snow and stared at the "hump".

It was a body "but of what nationality we couldn't tell. It had no headdress, no boots and was lying face downwards on the tracks. As it was frozen stiff to the tracks we couldn't turn it. Out of respect for the dead we didn't want to disturb him. We didn't know if he was a British paratrooper, an American soldier or a German ... No marks on the back, head not smashed, feet in good condition – we couldn't see where he had been hit."[6]

They left him and continued with their patrol. The "hump" disappeared into the falling snow. Perhaps someone found it again later. Dunkley never knew. Shortly afterwards he was evacuated to the UK, having lost his right leg.

For most of the "Nijmegen Home Guard" the most lasting memories of that freezing terrible winter were the rusting remains of the great battle that had been fought there the previous September. Jack Frame, another nineteen-year-old Yorkshireman with the 49th, remembers today: "Only the jeeps, the trucks, the bits and pieces of equipment that were scattered everywhere, some of it looking as if it were still in working order. Now and again you'd come across something which looked too tempting – a pair of binoculars or a pistol. But by then we'd got to know that old Jerry was a cunning sod. He'd booby-trap anything that looked tempting. So you kept your hands off such things – if you wanted to keep your hands, like."[7]

Occasionally the "cunning sods" would venture across the Rhine and the flooded fields to do a little patrolling of their own. On January 15th a patrol of the Hallamshire Regiment out on the Island found a group of wrecked houses, previously empty but now occupied, with barbed wire strung around them – and the new tenants were obviously drunk. One of them shouted through the window at the stalled British infantry: "English good soldiers!"

A moment later another drunken German called after him: "*Ja –* German better still!"

The latter proved more correct. That night the Hallamshires got a bloody nose and the Germans moved away the victors.

Two days later, another patrol challenged a body of men moving through the icy darkness in the traditional English manner: "Halt, who goes there?"

The answer barked back across the hundred yards separating the two groups caused no little surprise. It was a guttural "*Schmidt!*"

So it had gone all winter, day for day, week for week, month for month. The Yorkshiremen's only respite was the few hours they got at Nijmegen where they went dancing – and even then they carried their weapons. A few, a very fortunate few, managed to acquire a pass for thirty-six hours in Brussels with its palatial "Montgomery Club" and the whores in the Rue Neuve and behind the railway station.

The Island was a backwater of the war and the men of the 49th had really settled in there to become a true "Home Guard"; while all those long months of the coldest winter within living memory, the spires and towers of Arnhem lay on the horizon to the north, a kind of mocking tidemark of the invasion year: so temptingly close, yet in reality as far away as the moon itself.

But soon the "Nijmegen Home Guard" would be activated again. After six months of semi-idleness they would go into action one last time. Now once more, as March approached its end, Montgomery was preparing to "bounce the Rhine" one final time. Their days on the Island were numbered. The Canadian I Corps would attack across the Rhine from Germany into Holland and the 49th Infantry Division would play a vital part in that attack. Its target would be Arnhem itself.

THREE

The plan envisaged General Foulkes' I Canadian Corps, to which the 49th Division belonged, invading Holland from Germany by crossing the Rhine at the border town of Emmerich. Meanwhile, supported by the Canadian 5th Armoured Division, the 49th would attack and capture Arnhem itself.

General Foulkes' Intelligence was a little vague on what to expect on the other side. They knew that the attackers were vastly outnumbered by the Germans of General Blaskowitz's 120,000-strong Twenty-fifth Army; but they had little idea of the quality of the opposition. One thing they did know: the men who attacked Arnhem would be fighting Dutch SS men. Ironically enough, the second battle of Arnhem would be fought against the very people whom those ill-fated paras of the British 1st Airborne Division had believed they were coming to liberate back in September 1944!

Montgomery had thought the Canadian troops fighting their first actions in Normandy were "a bit jumpy". Now he had learned just how strong the fighting qualities the average Canadian soldier were. With three hundred per cent casualties in their rifle companies since Normandy, they had paid the butcher's bill to the full.

But some of their staffs had still not settled down and were not as professional as comparable staffs in the British Army. As the Canadian historian Colonel Stacey noted of them at that time: "The Canadians would have done better if they had not been learning the business as they fought ... A proportion of officers were not fully competent for their appointments and their inadequacy sometimes had serious consequences."[1]

General Foulkes, then commanding the 2nd Canadian Infantry

Division, was even franker: "When we went into action at Falaise and Caen we found that when we bumped into battle-experienced German troops we were no match for them ... It took two months to get the Division so shaken down that we were really a machine who could fight."[2]

But even now, six months later, General Foulkes' staff were still undecided on how to attack Arnhem effectively, although they had had nearly two months to make their plans. As one British officer who would go in with the first wave of the assault infantry of the 49th Division, Lieutenant E. Burkart of the 2nd Glosters, noted after the war in his regimental magazine: "At the risk of being thought frivolous, I would remind readers that this was a battle that very nearly did not come off ... Higher Authority seemed quite unable to decide how to attack Arnhem."[3]

On April 7th, after at least four changes of plans, the 1st Canadian Corps finally made up its mind. The 49th Division would cross the Lower Rhine near Doornenburg and move from there to Westervoort. This meant they would attack Arnhem from the east and, the planners hoped, would thus catch the defenders off guard; for it seemed the Germans were expecting the Allied attack to come from the south.

Now the operation went into full swing, as engineers prepared pre-fabricated bridges and others readied special mine-removing equipment, bull-dozers, breakdown trucks, and all the rest of the gear needed by a mechanized army on the move.

To the rear of the waiting infantry and the busy sappers, the Canadian staff got down to the rarified details of planning stop lines, start lines, schwerpunkts, TOTs, etcetera. Everything was being carefully prepared and timed down to the split second. In the event, nearly everything went wrong.

Now the infantry commanders of the "Nijmegen Home Guard", going into action again after so long, began to reconnoitre their objectives for the day. Together with the brigade group of the Division's 5th Brigade, the CO of the 7th Duke of Wellington's crept forward under cover of smoke towards the Rhine.

The plan was for the infantry colonels and their brigadier to use the cover of thick white smoke spurting from the huge generators until they reached some abandoned trenches from the previous September's fighting. Once there, the smoke screen would stop for an hour while the Group lay quietly in the trenches, carrying out a textbook reconnaissance.

The CO of the Duke of Wellingtons was quite thrilled at his proposed objective. For it was to be the Hartenstein Hotel, where the "Big General" and what was left of his paras had made "their last dramatic stand in September 1944."[4]

But the party never reached the old trenches. They were only halfway there when the smoke started to peter out; the engineers had got their timing wrong. "Everything from Spandaus to a far-away railway gun opened up." Leaving the rest of his fellow COs to their fate, the colonel of the Wellingtons pelted for the safety of a boathouse, already sheltering two Canadian snipers. For an hour the three of them laughed themselves hoarse at the antics of the other senior officers; for every time they attempted to move, the Germans on the other side of the river opened up at them. In the end, however, they did manage to escape and joined the three in the boathouse. Now a thin haze of fresh smoke started to drift over their side of the Rhine and the colonels decided to make a run for it over 2,000 yards of completely open, flooded potato fields.

They had hardly started when the wind promptly changed, wafting the smoke away and revealing their presence. The Germans were "clearly puzzled by this behaviour", but they needed no second invitation to open fire at this strange bunch of senior Tommy officers dodging around to whatever purpose in no man's land. The colonels fled for their lives. It was to be one of the many "snafus" which dogged the second battle of Arnhem...

On the morning of April 12th the whole weight of the 1st Canadian Corps' artillery fell on Arnhem. With startling suddenness, the half-deserted town was woken that Thursday dawn by the thunder of the Canadians' multiple rocket guns. One of these "mattresses", as the massed rockets were called, was the equivalent of the guns of a whole regiment of artillery! But not only were the professional artillerymen engaged; any type of spare gun from mortar to tank-mounted machine gun was pressed into service, too. The whole left bank of the Rhine was soon ablaze. As one eye-witness recalled: "It was so inspiring and yet frightening that I remember we could not talk but just stood and watched."[5]

Now the Typhoons and other fighter-bombers arrived, many of them flying from fields deep in Germany by this time. Zooming low beneath the German flak they roared in at 400 mhp, machine guns blazing, deadly rockets hissing from beneath their wings, a myriad black lethal eggs dropping from their bellies.

On and on the guns thundered as the planes raced away, soaring into the clear blue sky to escape the smoke, leaving death and destruction behind them. Now as H-Hour approached – 10.40 pm that Thursday – their faces stinging from the repeated blast waves and their ears already deafened, the gunners increased the volume of their fire. Every minute they pumped five shells per gun at the defenders. "*IN!*" the harsh command and the metallic snap of the breach closing. "*FIRE!*" the hoarse bellow. The slap of the hot acrid air across their sweat-glazed faces and the hollow rattle of the empty brass shell-case dropping on the pile at their feet. Over and over again. As the storm boats and the great lumbering Buffaloes came in to ferry the lead brigade across, one field gun battery of eight guns fired 640 rounds in ten minutes – more shells than they would have been allowed in a whole year's training in peace-time! But at this critical moment no one thought of the cost. The infantry were going in. Human lives counted more than the price of ammunition.

Now the Glosters, the men of the South Wales Borderers, and Essexs of the 56th Infantry Brigade, which would lead the assault, started to move out in their Buffaloes and storm boats, their way lit by "Monty's Moonlight", Bofors guns firing tracer to indicate the right direction over their heads.

It had been intended that the craft should sail through a gap blown in the embankment by the engineers. This would ensure that the Buffaloes and storm boats were not exposed on the height to enemy fire. The charges had duly been laid, twenty-four hours before. Now the sappers pressed their detonator boxes – but instead of the tremendous explosion they expected, the huge gap in the concrete and earth construction that would allow the craft to pass through straight into the water, there came a few feeble stutters, a fizzle of sparks, faint puffs of smoke. The explosives had failed to go off!

As Burkart of the Glosters commented afterwards: "The carefully laid plans went wrong. It is a credit to the careful briefing and determined responsibility of platoon commanders that the assault was made at all."[6]

But the Glosters' attack was floundering. By now they had discovered that their assault boats were defective; instead of a four-company attack, they were going to be forced to ferry their companies across one at a time. The second battalion of the assault brigade, the South Wales Borderers, began crossing under fire. The current began to seize their craft. To his horror their CO saw that his battalion was going to land far away from the intended spot. But there was nothing he could do about it now. The first of his craft hit the opposite bank and immediately ran into trouble: some of the Buffaloes could not climb the steep embankment, and as their ramps inexplicably wouldn't open, the Borderers had to jump twelve feet to the ground in full view of the Germans!

Cursing and furious with rage, the CO pushed his men forward up the road which led to Arnhem. A small group of Germans trying to hold them up with a light machine gun were forced to retreat. The Borderers' pace quickened. They all had read how the paras' attack in the September of the previous year had failed because they had not reached Arnhem in sufficient strength before the SS could react. They were not going to let that happen this April. But again luck was against the "Nijmegen Home Guard". As Private Hollins, who was with the Borderers, recalled after the war: "I was in the leading section of the leading company and as we came under a railway bridge, with open ground to our left and a row of houses to our right, we were pinned down by LMG fire and took refuge in the houses."[7]

The South Wales Borderers would remain in those houses for the next twelve hours. Already it seemed the 49th Infantry attack on Arnhem was beginning to bog down.

They called it the "Gremlin", which seemed only appropriate to those who now realized that this whole operation was bugged by gremlins.[8] It was the Royal Engineers' name for the folding pre-fabricated boat bridge that they had been building this past week. This contraption was devised to carry the tanks of the 5th Canadian Armoured Division across the river near Doornenburg.

While the 2nd Glosters were behind in their timing and were hurrying – regardless – through enemy minefields to reach their objective on time, the 5th were *ahead* of schedule. It was another "snafu" – only this particular "snafu" could lead to disaster, for if the Shermans of the 5th reached the other side across the "gremlin" bridge to find that there was no infantry to protect them, all hell would break loose. The tanks would be sitting ducks; the German infantry armed with their dreaded rocket-launchers, the *panzerfaust*, would be able to knock off the Shermans with impunity.

After all the preparation, the inner steeling of nerves, the tension of the pre-battle situation, the men of the Duke of Wellington's Regiment now feared that it had been all for nothing. As the regimental history put it: "It looked doubtful if the Battalion was to play any active part in the operation."[9]

Then it was learned that the attack of the South Wales Borderers had bogged down on the other side. The Wellingtons would have to go to their aid and help them open up a vital set of roads. That night they would cross the river, infiltrate through Arnhem, and link up with the Borderers to the north of the railway station.

A training manual of those days maintained: "For night attacks one requires hours, if not days, of preparation. The troops must be rested and properly briefed. If possible, there should be a rehearsal over similar ground."[10] But in this case the briefing was dealt with in a matter of minutes; the Wellingtons' A company under a Captain Kilner had to set off at once, with orders to provide a firm base and a protective screen for the rest of the battalion. There was only one catch. The South Wales Borderers were not where they were supposed to be; and Kilner's radio link to brigade headquarters had broken down, so he couldn't even ask brigade staff where the Borderers were now. Again – *snafu!*

But fortunately on that long hard day, one thing did go according to plan. The 2nd Glosters, after the loss of 32 men killed or wounded, eventually managed to reach the spot where the floating bridge would be emplaced *one minute* before it came out of the fog of war, its motors chugging merrily, the sappers crouching warily on its swaying decks. Half an hour later the river was spanned and the tanks of the 5th Canadian Armoured Division began to roll across into Arnhem – followed by those most fearsome weapons of all, the flame-throwing Crocodiles of the British 79th Armoured Division. The last phase of the second battle of Arnhem was about to commence.

FOUR

That morning one of the few civilians to remain in the shattered city, which in the last few months had been the victim of German V-2s that had fallen short, Mevrouw Riggeling, ventured out into the embattled streets to see what was going on.

As she approached the Amsterdammer Weg she spotted the first Canadian tanks rolling into battle. She also saw something else: a dead German soldier sprawled out in a pool of blood on the pavement.

The fifty-year-old Dutchwoman, a pious churchgoer, bent and removed the dead man's helmet; then, thinking the body might well be looted, as had the bodies of the dead paras back in the previous September, she removed the German's wallet for safe-keeping.

Something made her open it and a snapshot fell out – a picture of "a young woman with three girls between six and eight". On it was scrawled in a childish hand: "*Auf Wiedersehen, Papa*".

Mevrouw Riggeling was near to tears as she thought of those children who had just – unknown to them – lost their father for good. Silently she began to pick some flowers that grew at the end of the road. When she had collected a little bunch she laid them near the dead German, whispering: "In the name of your wife and children..." Then she said the Lord's Prayer for him.

"I always remember that dead German," she said, many years later, "and am glad that I acted as I did. I shall never forget that morning in Arnhem."[1]

She was not the only one. As the infantry and Canadians battled to wrest Arnhem from its German and Dutch defenders, Captain Wilson and his Crocodiles crossed the Rhine not far from the spans "of the great steel bridge which the Parachute Brigade had fought so hard to hold". He found everywhere the relics of that old battle, mixed with those of the new. "Parachutes hung from the trees. Containers lay open where they had fallen to the ground. At one place [we] came on a burnt-out jeep. At another the wreck of a British six-pounder; beside it was a pile of empty shell-cases and a group of wooden crosses. Before they had died the gunners had scored an epic victory. Across the road were two old French "Char B" tanks used by the Dutch SS. Both had been knocked out by the same shot."[2]

Veteran of the long campaign as he was, Captain Wilson was awed and not a little frightened by what he saw that day. "It was," he wrote later, "like entering an ancient tomb."

Reg Dunkley, one of the seven surviving members of his company who had landed in Normandy, felt the strange atmosphere of the place as well as he plodded through the ruined outskirts with the green replacements. "It was ghostly being in an empty town. You felt you had no right to be there and that someone was watching you in case you did something you shouldn't. You were looking over your shoulder all the time. The other lads felt it too."[3]

But there were a few lighter moments, too, in the midst of the confused fighting for the Dutch city, as more and more Canadian tanks came up to help the hard-pressed British infantry. For a few hours that day the men of the Duke of Wellington's Regiment became the involuntry custodians of the city's zoo.

The day before, one of the zoo's precious elephants "had succumbed to shell shock", as the regimental magazine noted later. But, despite a shortage of rations, there were still plenty of exotic animals left and Major Gerald Fancourt, who was now in charge, called his Brigadier on the air and offered him a swop. If the Brigadier would let him have the little wooden model of the divisional sign which he kept in his caravan he'd send up the real thing – "*a very live and hungry polar bear!*"[4]

The offer was not accepted.

Later that same day the Duke of Wellingtons, holding a crossroads they had taken over from the South Wales Borderers, were astonished to see a whole company of German soldiers accompanied by three French-built Renault tanks heading straight towards them. Evidently the Germans did not know the crossroads was held by the Yorkshiremen. But they soon found out. The Battalion's D Company dealt with them with "little difficulty", as the regimental history put it, and the prisoners soon confirmed that "they had no idea the Battalion was there".

It was almost too easy. As Captain MacDonald of the Canadian 11th Armoured Regiment commented: "By 1945 we were the professionals and the Germans were the amateurs. They were using boys of sixteen and so on. They were not what they had been and they knew the war was over too."[5]

But there were still some among the German troops, green as they might be, who would fight to the end. They had no choice. Whether they surrendered or fought on, they knew their fate would be the same – death in battle or death at the hands of a firing squad. They were the Dutch SS.

Like all the rest of Europe's youth which had flocked to join the SS in the good years,[6] the reasons for these young tall Dutchmen volunteering for the Black Guards were varied. Some were simply naive. Some were opportunists, greedy to climb aboard the bandwagon of the "Greater Germany". Some were adventurers, eager for the excitement and glamour of that black-clad formation with its silver runes and skull-and-crossbones badge.

But these young Dutch volunteers of 1945 had not experienced the shock of the Russian front like their instructors. The "Soviet subhumans" were not the cowards they had been taught they were. In Russia in the middle years of the war the SS – "the Bodyguard", the "Death's Head", the "Viking", and all the rest of those units with their bold, defiant names – had been bled white. Those who had escaped that blood-bath for the quieter pastures of Occupied Holland had been brutalized by their experiences, but they had grown wise. They were the ones who, when the Allies broke through at Arnhem, quietly abandoned their units, found civilian clothes, and "took a dive", in their parlance, hoping to save their skins.

Behind them they left the callow youths they had trained. Now these green young SS men found themselves fighting skilled soldiers, who were just as brutalized as their departed instructors had been. Swiftly they learned that April there was no use surrendering. The British and the Canadians were not taking prisoners that month – if they happened to be Dutch and SS as well.

Canadian Lieutenant Leo Heaps had been one of the paras who had managed to escape from the débâcle at Arnhem the previous September. All winter long he had been helping MI9, the British escape organization, to bring back those of the paras who were still on the run or in hiding in Holland. Now at last he was back where he started – Arnhem. Together with a jeep squadron of the SAS under the command of Major Henry Druce, he had crossed the Rhine and was now located at a crossroads north-west of the city.

Suddenly the stationary jeeps and some Shermans of the 5th Canadian Armoured Division came under a severe artillery barrage. The tankers disappeared instantly into the safety of their turrets. But there was no sheltering in the open jeeps, and as Heaps recorded: "Henry didn't mind being *behind* the lines, but being in front of the enemy was an entirely new proposition!"[7] So the SAS men turned and raced down a side road at breakneck speed with "the shells whining over our heads and then crashing on the crossroads".

Finally they felt themselves safe; the SAS halted and sent out a patrol to find out where the opposition was. It wasn't very far: just up the road, in fact. The tough SAS men, who had operated behind German lines in France for *five months* before the invasion had started the previous year, returned with "half a dozen Germans who were found indifferently laying telephone cable ... They were happy to be taken prisoner."

But one of the other prisoners was not happy at all. He was a Dutch civilian, tall and slim, with the look of a soldier about him. Eric, Major Druce's Dutch interpreter, went to work on him immediately. Major Druce watched impassively; he had seen it all before in his long years working with the Resistance. Obviously the Dutchman, frantically pleading with the interpreter, was a traitor of some kind.

Druce was right. The Dutchman was a member of the *SS Nederland*, attempting to escape in civilian clothes. He started to blab out his "confession".

Eric didn't give him a chance. "Without a moment's hesitation he picked up one of the SAS's silenced Sten-guns from the nearest jeep and shoved the terrified SS man in front of him to the back of the nearest house."[8]

There was a muffled burst and Eric returned, face set and grim, having shot the SS man. Moments later, two of the SAS took up their shovels and silently began to bury the traitor.

It was not surprising that the SS fought to the death.

And they made the Canadians and the British pay that day in Arnhem too. The Duke of Wellington's Regiment had about cleared all the day's objectives when SS men of the *Nederland* launched a counter-attack on its D Company. It was beaten off, but only after a sharp skirmish in which the enemy's light tanks were knocked out. Now Private Reg Dunkley's section was called upon to recce the woods to the front from which the Dutch counter-attack had come. All the men in the section were veterans – the oldest serving members of the Battalion who had been with it since Normandy. The rest were replacements.

"So off we went, seven of us in line abreast," Dunkley recalled many years later, "mostly armed with automatics ... Object: to pin-point any positions dug in the woods. We had gone about 150 yards when the stonk opened up ... just like that. A distinct whistle of shells. No word of command was given to retreat. ... We just turned 180 degrees and ran like the dickens."9

The sergeant in charge fell, killed by the same shell that hit Dunkley. "I knew I was wounded. There was a singing and ringing in my ears. I knew my right kneecap had gone. You know at the dentist you can feel the grating of the instrument on the bone – so I could feel my kneecap grating; and it wouldn't go where I wanted it to. I couldn't speak and I thought I'd bought it." He tried to shout to one of his comrades, only a few yards away, "but I could make no sounds. So I scrambled myself along to a sapling and propped my back against it so that I was partly upright and visible to anyone walking near by."

How long he lay there Reg Dunkley never knew. Suddenly he heard someone say: "Let's get Dunkley away first. The sergeant's obviously gone for a chop." The stretcher-bearers had found him. "I felt no pain, I was so numb or senseless, but when the stretcher-bearers put me on the stretcher I lost consciousness."

Those unknown SS men had put an end to the fighting career of yet another Allied soldier. Dunkley was evacuated home to the UK, having lost his right leg above the knee.

Now it was almost over in Arnhem. War correspondent Matthew Halton of the CBC, who had followed the troops across the river, felt it was somehow appropriate "that it should be a British formation, the 49th West Riding Division, that should take Arnhem at long last and write the words 'Paid in Full' across another page of British history. Last September the world stopped breathing to watch this town. If the British Army had been able to link hands with the British 1st Airborne which had landed at Arnhem, the Rhine would have been turned while the German armies were disorganized and the armoured divisions would have poured into the plains of Hanover and Westphalia."[10]

But that, of course, had not happened. As a result, Arnhem had suffered its second battle within six months – "a deserted, burning shell" Halton called it now as he wandered through the city streets. "Fires were blazing. Machine guns chattered . . . two or three German shells whistled in . . . The whole thing was a dreary disheartening sight."

Halton met a lone Dutchman coming slowly down a long street. He shook hands with the correspondent and said quietly: "You have come back." Nothing more.

Halton had had enough. He drove away from this sad, mad place. "There were craters everywhere. White tapes through the minefields. A British soldier who had lost a foot on a Schu-mine. Two others being buried. Engineers making demolitions. Bulldozers backing up a few feet, shaking their heads in a roaring anger and then tearing into the side of a broken house. A Martian ant-hill . . . a bedlam of men at the war. Motor cycles bouncing back and forth. Tanks and Bren-carriers dusting through to the next battle. Convoy leaders going crazy to get their convoys through. All the noisy clanking machines and paraphernalia of war."

The Germans and their Dutch allies attempted one last counter-attack. One day after the suburbs of Arnhem had at last been cleared, Druce's SAS group in their armoured jeeps, each of them carrying *five* machine guns, had stopped for a hurried meal in a wood. Suddenly there was the bellowing of German voices and the sound of horse-drawn transport close by. There was a sharp scuffle, then silence. The SAS had captured a stray German. Hurriedly interrogated by Eric, the prisoner answered their questions smartly enough, and the little SAS group discovered to their horror that they had somehow ended up between two German regiments who were going to counter-attack the Canadians' forward elements at nearby Otterloo.

Druce decided this was no place to linger. They loaded their prisoner into a jeep and decided to make a dash for it. It was nearly dark, with only a bit of a moon shining through the thick clouds, and Druce hoped this would provide them with the cover they needed. Boldly the column of jeeps moved onto the road out of the woods, the muzzle of a Sten gun stuck in the German's skinny ribs to keep him quiet.

Soon they saw the dim outlines of the Germans advancing along the road to Otterloo to attack the Canadians. Druce's driver put his foot down on the accelerator. The jeep shot forward. Now they were level with the Germans. Obligingly they moved closer to the edge of the road to let Druce's jeep by. Another jeep followed and another. Not a single shot was fired. Once again, the SAS had proved the truth of their motto: *"He who dares wins!"*

A Canadian sergeant of the artillery challenged the infiltrators first. His answer came back in a vicious burst of spandau fire. The gunners needed no other warning. They leapt into action. Even as tracer fire started to zip towards them they grabbed for their shells.

The Germans were already so close that it was a matter of firing over open sights. Within minutes the excited German infantry had swamped the Canadian positions. But the gunners did not give up, even though the Germans were already streaming into Otterloo itself. They dug themselves in and fought back with Stens, rifles and pistols. Grimly they hung on; not one of them surrendered, nor did they lose a single gun.

Now it was the turn of the Canadians of the 5th Armoured Division in this "Battle of Otterloo" as Matthew Halton of CBC later called it. One Canadian colonel, crouching below his caravan like some Wild West pioneer in a wagon-train attacked by Indians, killed two of the German attackers. Nearby, his batman knocked off three. As Halton reported later: "Nearly everybody in the headquarters has at least one notch to carve on his gun. Some have as many as ten!"[11]

It was brutal and unfeeling, the slaughter at Otterloo that April 16th, 1945, but after all, those who fought led short and brutish lives; they could not afford the luxury of sentiment or compassion. So they shot down the desperate Germans in their shabby field-grey uniforms and carved another notch on the butts of their weapons like the western gunslingers they had seen in the movies back home.

At the height of that desperate battle for the obscure Dutch town, four Bren-gun carriers adapted to fire flame – Wasps, as they were known – came rattling up just as another group of Germans were preparing to attack along the main street. They had arrived just in time; the heavily outnumbered defenders were weakening. Hurriedly the Wasps swung into action. "Great tongues of flame spurted out," Halton reported. "Terrible screams came from those who did not die instantly. In front of one flame-thrower this morning I saw 105 German dead, all terribly burned."

Those deadly Wasps turned the tide. The last German attack fell apart and the survivors started to withdraw like timber-wolves deprived of their prey, slinking back into the forest from whence they had come.

The Canadians of the 5th Armoured Division had broken them. "With 400 German dead," Walton told his listeners, "and 250 taken prisoner, the remnants of the German force are being rounded up in the woodlands around Otterloo. Man for man those gunners and headquarters' soldiers had outfought the Germans. They killed more of the enemy than I have ever seen in such a small area."

And in the fields and among the smouldering blackened rubble of the little town, there they lay. Shrunken, charred pygmies, skeletal faces contorted with searing agony, spines arched as they tried in vain to ward off that terrible all-consuming flame, their hands stiffened to claws like the branches of an ancient withered tree. Fresh tribute this murderous April to man's inhumanity to man . . .

As the fighting around Arnhem started to die down the third brigade of the 49th Division, the 147th, began to move up to the wooded area beyond, where at this moment Reg Dunkley lay severely wounded, waiting to be picked up.

In the lead were the 1st Leicesters, heading for the high ground. Among the men of the company at point was Private Bob Day, twenty-one years old, who had already been wounded the previous year at the Salerno landings in Italy. Day and the platoon Bren-gunner had just reached a small dell when there was a "dreadful shrieking sound followed by a tremendous bang".

Day flung himself to the ground. For what seemed an age but in reality was only a mere minute, fist-sized, glowing fragments of steel hissed back and forth among the trees, slicing down anything that lay in their path. As Day recalled later: "It was far worse than any mortar fire I had encountered".

Then mercifully the mortar bombardment ceased. Cautiously Day raised himself, hardly daring to believe that he was still alive. Suddenly his ears were assailed by screams coming from the other side of the smoking dell, its surface now scarred by the steaming brown pits made by the mortar bombs. An officer was swaying back and forth, his ashen young face contorted in agony, screaming high and hysterical like a woman, holding an arm which had been nearly severed, the bright red blood seeping through his tightly clenched fingers.

"The poor chap was obviously delirious," Day remembered after the war, "and several of my section did what they could to comfort him before he was taken away on a stretcher."[12]

Day watched him being borne away, his blood dripping on to the grass; then he turned to have a word with the Bren-gunner who had accompanied him into the dell. To his surprise he still was lying there against a bank, his head bent forward as if he were asleep, strangely unaffected by the drama and tragedy of the last few minutes. Day frowned and nudged the young gunner. But he was dead. There was a tiny hole at the back of his head and Day concluded that "he must have been killed instantly".

The irony of it all was that the young soldier had not been killed by enemy guns but by rockets from one of the Canadian "mattresses".

"I cannot remember his name," Day recalled many years later, "but he was a quiet pleasant fellow who had told me only a day or so previously that his wife had had a baby."[13]

In the moment of victory, yet another young man had died violently, never again to see the wife he had loved or the baby he had sired...

FIVE

Back in that September of 1944 when it had all started, the veteran *kriegies* of the RAF prisoner-of-war camp at Fallingbostel in Northern Germany, some of whom had been there since 1940, had witnessed a sight that made them proud to be British.

They already knew, thanks to their secret radio – code-named "Canary" for obvious reasons – all about the 1st Airborne Division's epic stand at Arnhem. Now the whole camp turned out and pressed themselves against the wire, under the hard-eyed gaze of their guards, to watch the first para-prisoners pass.

"They were marched along the road past our camp by RSM Lord," one of the RAF prisoners, Sergeant John Dominy, recalled. "He had the swagger of a Guardsman on parade. They were carrying their wounded and their guards were a shambling dishevelled lot, just about keeping pace with the steady Praetorian tread of the finest soldiers in the world."[1]

The RAF men did not cheer. Instinctively they came to attention in silent salute to the brave men who had survived Arnhem.

RSM Lord, six foot two and a former Grenadier Guardsman, noticed the RAF's two medical officers standing there among the watchers out of the corner of his eye. "Party – *eyes right!*" he barked and swung the two MOs a salute that wouldn't have been out of place in the Guards depot in peacetime.

As Dominy commented: "This was the sort of show England could really put on. The impression on the Germans was incredible."

Thus RSM Lord and his "Red Devils" had entered the lives of the 7,000 British, Canadian and American prisoners at Fallingbostel, some 1,000 of them in the *lazarett*, the camp hospital, suffering from wounds and malnutrition. He found them not only feeling defeated, but *looking* defeated. Dirty and scruffy for the most part, they stole from their comrades and were deep into all sorts of rackets. Morale and discipline were virtually nil.

Lord started on the barracks allotted to his own men first. Once he was satisfied with them, he began on the other units. In record time he had everyone shaving and washing regularly. "After that," as Dominy noted, "he looked around for French, Belgians and others with patent soldierly qualities. Within a week he had them organized as well."[2]

Private James Sims, the nineteen-year-old para who had been wounded at Arnhem, was one of those who had landed up in Fallingbostel's overcrowded *lazarett*. He summed it up thus: The British and Canadians were lucky in that they had RSM Lord ... He created order out of chaos, gave us back our self-respect, treated the Germans with contempt and bullied them into improving conditions ... There is no doubt that without this fine soldier there would have been more British graves in Stalag XIB than there were."[3]

Thus it was that, as the second battle of Arnhem came to an end on that bloody Monday of April 16th, 1945, and a squadron of tanks from the 7th Armoured Division's 8th Irish Hussars set out to liberate Stalag XIB, they were in for a great surprise.

While the infantrymen of the Queen's Regiment still battled it out with the German defenders in Fallingbostel itself, fighting from house to house against determined German resistance, the Hussars came trundling down the approach road to the great sprawling camp, the gunners tensed and ready for any kind of trouble, only to find the camp already in British hands!

Most of the German guards had departed the previous Friday and, in characteristic fashion, RSM Lord had immediately taken over. Only sixty armed German soldiers had been left to guard the 20,000 men of all nationalities – and they soon found themselves sharing the task with British paratroopers. Now they too were disarmed. The astonished Hussars were greeted at the camp gates by armed sentries from the 1st Airborne Division "immaculate in scrubbed belts and gaiters", as the historian of the 7th Armoured described them. "Inside were ten thousand British and American prisoners commanded by Regimental Sergeant Major Lord of the 1st Airborne, who was busily engaged in his office giving peace-time orders to his Orderly Warrant Officers!"[4]

Chester Wilmot, the Australian war correspondent, who had followed the Hussars into Fallingbostel, was angered at the way some of the POWs had been treated. "I saw them in hospital – drawn, haggard, starved – starved beyond description; limbs like matchsticks, bodies shrunken till their bones stood out like knuckles." But, Wilmot went on, "I saw also something that was inspiring and encouraging. All this German oppression and brutality and starvation hadn't been able to kill the spirit and self-respect of these men of Arnhem."[5]

He told his listeners back home on the BBC: "They'd managed to rise above their sordid environment and today those of them who were on guard or on duty were as soldierly in their bearing as they were the day they were captured. They were proud that they had had their own camp running when our tanks got there. They felt they had almost liberated themselves. And this afternoon they had the supreme pleasure of watching their German guards being marched away to our own prison cage. And as they watched they cheered."[6]

RSM Lord, who had undergone all the horrors of that first battle of Arnhem (he had been the "Big General's" self-appointed bodyguard), had every reason to be proud of his "Red Devils". They had ended as they had begun – as soldiers. After six hard months since Montgomery had declared so lightly that he would "bounce the Rhine", the survivors had triumphed. The "spirit of Arnhem" lived on.

One American officer watching them that day exclaimed in wonder: "*Prisoners? Gee, I thought they were troops going into the line!*"

On that same day, the "broken-down ex-cavalryman" was busily packing. He had just received a telephone message from London that British and Canadian troops had broken out from Arnhem. The people who had hidden him for so long were free at last. Swiftly he got together the various bundles of tea and coffee, donated from their rations by his friends in Rutland; there were tinned goods too, and presents and all the things he had borrowed from his Dutch friends, including his fabled "parti-coloured woollen underpants" to be returned.

Hours later he was flying home over the Channel, reading the last few lines of *Paradise Lost* which depict Michael leading the first man and woman away from Paradise:

The world was all before them, where to choose
Thir place of rest, and Providence thir guide:
They hand in hand with wandering steps and slow
Through Eden took thir solitarie way.

It seemed to him a particularly apt ending for himself and all those who had flown out with him so confidently on that bright September Sunday morning – and survived. Brigadier Hackett, "the broken-down ex-cavalryman", was returning to Arnhem. The wheel had turned full circle. It was victory on the Rhine at last.

ENVOI

> Christ – of course we would have done it again!
> Ex-Private "Mick" Tucker, 2nd Battalion
> 1st British Airborne Division, 1973

As April ended and World War Two dragged to its final close, the French at Speyer on the Rhine started to erect a monument to Sergeant Bertout and his ten North Africans who had crossed the great river in their rubber dinghy the month before.

It was in the form of a stone pillar, the height of a man. It bore the palm twig of the French Army, a curved scimitar, and some letters in Arabic, perhaps to symbolize French and Algerian co-operation.

Beneath, chiselled into the belly of the stone, there was the inscription:

> *Le 31 mars 1945 le 3⁰ Rgt de Tirailleurs*
> *Algériens franchit le Rhin*
> *L'operation fut executée par le groupe Franc*
> *du Regiment le 1er Battaillon et les Sappeurs*
> *de la 83/I Cie.*

It was to be a lasting tribute to the glory of France – and, naturally, to General Charles de Gaulle too.

In that terrible winter of 1944/45, thousands of Britons, Canadians and Americans died in the attempt to cross that same river. Yet for their effort and self-sacrifice there is no single monument, only the rows and rows of white headstones in those neat green cemeteries which trail across the battlefields of World War Two in North-West Europe. Along the whole length of the Rhine there is no trace of their passing. Only at Speyer, forty years later, does that weathered, grey stone still exist.[1]

So the Rhine flows on majestically with perhaps another legend to be added to all the rest – Attila the Hun; the Lorelei; Siegfried; the saga of the blond, bold Frank and his ten Moors who had battled across that March to brave the might of the Teuton single-handedly . . .

NOTES AND SOURCES

Introduction
1 Hackett, John, *I Came as a Stranger*, London, Fontana.
2 Interestingly enough, Lieutenant-Commander Ian Fleming, the creator of James Bond – "a real snake", in Winterbotham's words – tried to lure Cotton and his plane away to work for Naval Intelligence.

PART I: Defeat on the Rhine

Chapter One
1 Urquhart, Maj-Gen R. E. *Arnhem*, London, Cassell.
2 From an interview with the author.
3 Ibid.
4 Urquhart, op. cit.
5 Hagen, Louis, *Arnhem Lift*, London, Pilot Press.
6 Ibid.
7 Ibid.
8 Ibid.
9 Today Mr Hagen is an editor with a leading West German newspaper.
10 Maxted, *BBC War Report*.
11 Lloyd, Alan, *The Gliders*, Leo Cooper.
12 Ibid.
13 Ibid.
14 From a personal interview with the author.
15 From a personal interview with the author.
16 From a personal interview with the author.
17 Ryan, C, *A Bridge Too Far*, New York, Random House.
18 Urquhart, op. cit.
19 Ibid.

20 Gavin, James, *On To Berlin*, London, Leo Cooper.
21 Ryan, op. cit.
22 Bradley, Omar, *Soldier's Story*, New York, Simon & Schuster.
23 Ray, Cyril, *BBC War Report*.
24 Thompson, R. W. *Men under Fire*, London, Collins.

Chapter Two
 1 Maule, H. *Out of the Sands*, London, Corgi.
 2 Ibid.
 3 Ibid.
 4 Ibid.
 5 In his absence, Leclerc was sentenced to death by his fellow countrymen
    – like de Gaulle himself, who was similarly condemned by his own son's
    godfather, Marshal Pétain.
 6 Evans, op. cit.
 7 Ibid.
 8 Ibid.
 9 Ibid.
10 Ibid.
11 Day, Price, *BBC War Report*.
12 Evans, op. cit.
13 Ibid.
14 Ibid.
15 Ibid.
16 Vaughan Thomas, Wynford, *BBC War Report*.
17 Evans, op. cit.
18 Ibid.
19 Ibid.
20 Ibid.
21 Ibid.
22 Vaughan Thomas, op. cit.
23 Evans, op. cit.
24 Vaughan Thomas, op. cit.
25 Lieutenant Triumpho thus crossed the Rhine into Germany four months
    earlier than the first US officer officially recognized to do so, Lieutenant
    Timmermann at Remagen.
26 Evans, op. cit.

Chapter Three
 1 Thompson, R. W. *Men Under Fire*, London, MacDonald.
 2 Ibid.
 3 Ibid.
 4 Bradley, op. cit.

5 Ibid.
6 Ibid.
7 Ibid.
8 Ibid.
9 Ingersoll, R. *Top Secret*, London, Collins.

Chapter Four
1 Houston, D. *Hell on Wheels*, California, Presidio Press.
2 Ibid.
3 *Panzerfaust:* German rocket launcher.
4 Toland, John: *The Last Hundred Days*, New York, Random House.
5 Ibid.
6 Ibid.
7 Moorehead, Alan, *Eclipse*. London, Hamish Hamilton.
8 Ibid.
9 Twenty-three years later Moorehead's prediction was fulfilled in the Hollywood movie dramatizing the event, "A Bridge Too Far". (As a matter of interest, the film was made in Czechoslovakia just prior to the Russian invasion in 1968 – and the Russians made much of the presence of "armed" Americans, maintaining they had arrived to save this Eastern bloc country from a US takeover!)

PART II: The Most Famous Bridge in the World

Chapter One

1 As we have seen, this was not strictly true; Lieutenant Tony Triumpho had crossed the Rhine over four months previously.
2 Hechler, K. *The Bridge at Remagen*, New York, Ballantine.
3 Moorehead, op. cit.
4 McAlister, from correspondence with the author.
5 Hechler, op. cit.
6 Hechler, op. cit.
7 *Westwall:* German name for the Siegfried Line.
8 von Zangen, 15th German Army.
9 Toland, op. cit.
10 Ibid.
11 Ibid.
12 Ibid.
13 Those twin towers of the Remagen bridge now house a little museum commemorating the event. Predictably, perhaps, the walls are defaced with peace slogans and demands for "BREAD NOT WAR".
14 Toland, op. cit.
15 Ibid.

16 Timmermann's moment of glory was short-lived. Unwanted in his home town after the war, he rejoined the Army and went off to fight in Korea. Stricken by TB he died in a US veterans' hospital not long after his discharge, a forgotten man.

Chapter Two
1 Jodl, from an interview with Jodl's wife.
2 Toland, op. cit.
3 Toland, op. cit.
4 H. Butcher, *Three Years with Eisenhower*, London, Hutchinson.
5 Gavin, op. cit.
6 Churchill, as quoted from the *Daily Telegraph*, 1 April, 1945.
7 MacDonald, Dwight, from a personal interview with the author.
8 Farago, Ladislas, *Patton: Ordeal and Triumph*, New York, Ivan Obolensky.
9 Codman, Charles, *Drive!*, Boston, Atlantic Monthly Press.
10 Ibid.
11 Butcher, op. cit.

Chapter Three
1 Ayres, F., *Before the Colours Fade*, New York, Harper & Row.
2 Eisenhower, Dwight D., *Crusade in Europe*, London, Heinemann.
3 Farago, op. cit.
4 Codman, op. cit.
5 Eisenhower, op. cit.
6 Wellard, James, *Stars & Stripes*.
7 McKee, Alexander, *The Race for the Rhine Bridges*, London Souvenir Press.
8 Atwell, Private, from an interview with the author.
9 Ibid.

Chapter Four
1 Thompson, op. cit.
2 Ibid.
3 Brodie, from a letter to the author.
4 Highland Light Infantry Diary, 1945.
5 Sanders, St George, *Green Beret*, London, Four Square.
6 This figure includes the casualties of the 6th British Airborne Division, dropped on the second day.

Chapter Five
1 Codman, op. cit.
2 Ibid.

3 Ibid.
4 Ibid.
5 MacDonald, Charles B. *The Last Offensive*, Washington, US Army. [Official Publication.]
6 Codman, op. cit.
7 Ibid.
8 McKee, op. cit.
9 Ibid.
10 It was never used, however, for after the crossing there was no need for it.
11 Bradley, op. cit.
12 Ibid.
13 Ibid.

PART III: Victory on the Rhine

Chapter One
1 Schramm, Percy, *Wehrmachts-Beriche*, Heidelberg, 1950.
2 Ibid.
3 Ibid.
4 Ibid.
5 Wingfield, R. *The Only Way Out*, London, Hutchinson.
6 Goebbels, *Volkischer Beobachter*, 1945.
7 Kesselring, Albert, *Memoirs*, London, Collins.

Chapter Two
1 Whiting, Charles, *Finale at Flensburg*, London, Leo Cooper.
2 Ibid.
3 Ibid.
4 Ibid.
5 Ibid.
6 Ibid.
7 *A History of the Lincoln Regiment in World War II*, Aldershot, Gale & Polden.
8 McKee, op. cit.
9 Wilson, Andrew, *Flame Thrower*, London, Corgi.
10 Ibid.
11 Eisenhower, op. cit.
12 Horrocks, Brian, *A Full Life*, London, Leo Cooper.
13 Thompson, op. cit.
14 Cosgrave, from a personal interview with the author.
15 Thompson, op. cit.
16 Moorehead, op. cit.
17 Sanders, op. cit.
18 Ibid.

Chapter Three

1 *Hitler Speaks*, London, New English Library.
2 At the end of the war Raspe refused to surrender to anyone but the commander of the 51st. His wish was granted. Toland, op. cit.
3 Thomas, *BBC War Report*.
4 Prebble, from personal communication with the author.
5 McKee, op. cit.
6 Horrocks, op. cit.
7 McKee, op. cit.
8 Ibid.
9 Ibid.
10 Cosgrave, from a personal interview with the author.
11 Sanders, op. cit.
12 Ferguson, B. *The History of the Black Watch*, London, Collins.
13 McKee, op. cit.

Chapter Four

1 The Arnhem drop of three divisions took place over a whole week.
2 Lloyd, op. cit.
3 Whiting, op. cit.
4 Ibid.
5 Thompson, op. cit.
6 Moorehead, op. cit.
7 Lloyd, op. cit.
8 Ibid.
9 Ibid.
10 Maxted, *BBC War Report*.
11 Watts, *BBC War Report*.
12 Byrom, *BBC War Report*.
13 In a personal interview with the author, Captain Gill – or Major Gill, as he is now – told a bizarre story of how Montgomery personally sent him on a secret mission a few days prior to this airborne attack, flying across the Rhine to watch German troops movements. Forty years later he still stands by his story.
14 Colville, from a personal interview with the author.
15 Ibid.
16 Lloyd, op. cit.

Chapter Five

1 McKee, op. cit.
2 Ibid.
3 Ibid.
4 Ibid.

5 Ibid.
6 Ibid.
7 Ibid.
8 Ibid.
9 Ibid.
10 Ibid.
11 Ibid.
12 Ibid.
13 AP: armour-piercing shell.
14 *After Battle* Publications, London, 1970.
15 That colliery manager's house is now a hotel, appropriately named the *Rheinterrase Wacht am Berlin*.
16 Eisenhower, op. cit.
17 Bradley, op. cit.
18 After Battle, op. cit.
19 Ibid.
20 Eisenhower, op. cit.
21 Ibid.
22 Ibid.
23 Ibid.
24 Ibid.
25 Goebbels, J, *Tagebücher 1943–45*, Frankfurt, Bertelsmann.

Chapter Six
1 McKee, op. cit.
2 Ibid.
3 He was not the only German general to die that week on the Rhine. According to German sources, General Erdmann of the 7th Parachute Division committed suicide.
4 McKee, op. cit.
5 Anderson, D. *Three Cheers for the Next Man to Die*, London, Robert Hale.
6 McKee, op. cit.
7 Ibid.
8 HLI war diary, op. cit.
9 McKee, op. cit.
10 Thompson, op. cit.
11 Moorehead, op. cit.
12 McKee, op. cit.
13 Bedford, from a personal letter to the author.
14 Lloyd, op. cit.
15 Codman, op. cit.

16 Quoted in a letter written by General Bedell Smith to Eisenhower in 1948. Eisenhower, *Crusade in Europe*, op. cit.

17 Ryan, op. cit.

18 Monty as quoted in Lamb, Richard, *Montgomery In Europe 1943–45: Success or Failure*, London, Buchan & Enright.

PART IV: Return to Arnhem

Chapter One

1 Codman, op. cit.

2 Whiting, Charles, *The End of the War*, London, Leo Cooper.

3 Ibid.

Chapter Two

1 Ibid.

2 The French made two more crossings of the Rhine: at Leimersheim (April 2nd) and south of Strasbourg (April 15th). The latter was the last of all the assault crossings.

3 Stacy, E., *Maple Leaf Route*, London, Macmillan.

4 Tanner: a sixpence (pre-decimal coinage).

5 van der Zee, Henri from a letter to the author.

6 McKee, op. cit.

7 Frame, Jack, from a personal interview with the author.

Chapter Three

1 Stacey, op. cit.

2 Ibid.

3 McKee, op. cit.

4 Ibid.

5 Eye-witness account from a personal interview with the author.

6 McKee, op. cit.

7 Ibid.

8 "*Gremlin*" was RAF slang in World War Two for a persistant fault which developed in an aircraft and for which there seemed no rational explanation.

9 *A History of the Duke of Wellington's Regiment*, Aldershot, Ed. Gale & Polden.

Chapter Four

1 Riggeling, from personal correspondence with the author.

2 Wilson, op. cit.

3 McKee, op. cit.

4 Fancourt, from a personal interview with the author.

5 MacDonald, from a personal interview with the author.
6 Virtually every occupied country save Poland provided an SS unit, Indeed, the last SS man to win the Knight's Cross of the Iron Cross was a French soldier, from the SS Division *Charlemagne*, the French Unit that fought to the last in Berlin.
7 Heaps, Leo, *A Grey Goose at Arnhem*, London, Leo Cooper.
8 Ibid.
9 McKee, op. cit.
10 Ibid.
11 Ibid.
12 Ibid.
13 Ibid.

Chapter Five
1 Dominy, John, *The Sergeant Escapers*, London, Coronet.
2 Ibid.
3 Sims, James, *Arnhem Spearhead*, London, Sphere Books.
4 *Desert Rats: The 7th Armoured Division in World War II*. Privately published in Germany.
5 Wilmot, Chester, *The Struggle for Europe*, London, Collins.
6 Ibid.

ENVOI

1 My informant, the archives librarian at Speyer, writes that local legend claims there is another French memorial to the crossing at the mouth of the Old Rhine; but it has long since disappeared (if indeed it ever existed) into the thick Auwald Forest.

INDEX